Pride and His Prisoners

A. L. O. E.

BIBLIOLIFE

PRIDE AND HIS PRISONERS.

A. L. O. E.

Authoress of " The Young Pilgrim," " Flora," " The Giant-killer," " The " by Family,"
" Precepts in Practice," " Idols in the Heart," &c. &c.

"O! what have I to do with Pride!"—Sir W. Scott.

T. NELSON AND SONS, PATERNOSTER ROW;
EDINBURGH; AND NEW YORK.

MDCCCLX.

CONTENTS.

PRIDE AND HIS PRISONERS.

CHAPTER I.

THE HAUNTED DWELLING.

> " He who envies now thy state,
> Who now is plotting how he may seduce
> Thee also from obedience ; that with him,
> Bereaved of happiness, thou mavst partake
> His punishment,—eternal misery ! "   MILTON.

BRIGHT and joyous was the aspect of nature on a
spring morning in the beautiful county of Somersetshire. The budding green on the trees was yet so
light, that, like a transparent veil, it showed the out-
lines of every twig ; but on the lowlier hedges it lay
like a rich mantle of foliage, and clusters of prim-
roses nestled below, while the air was perfumed with
violets. Already was heard the hum of some adventurous bee in search of early sweets, the distant low
of cattle from the pasture, the mellow note of the

cuckoo from the grove,—every sight and sound told
of enjoyment on that sunny Sabbath morn.

Yet let me make an exception. There was one
spot which reserved to itself the unenviable privilege
of looking gloomy all the year round. Nettleby
Tower, a venerable edifice, stood on the highest summit of a hill, like some stern guardian of the fair
country that smiled around it. The tower had been
raised in the time of the Normans, and had then
been the robber-hold of a succession of fierce barons,
who, from their strong position, had defied the power
of king or law. The iron age had passed away.
The moat had been dried, and the useless portcullis
had rusted over the gate. The loop-holes, whence
archers had pointed their shafts, were half filled up
with the rubbish accumulated by time. Lichens had
mantled the grey stone till its original hue was almost
undistinguishable; silent and deserted was the court-
yard which had so often echoed to the clatter of
hoofs, or the ringing clank of armour.

Silent and deserted—yes! It was not time alone
that had wrought the desolation. Nettleby Tower
had stood a siege in the time of the Commonwealth,
and the marks of bullets might still be traced on its
walls; but the injuries which had been inflicted by
the slow march of centuries, or the more rapid visita-
tion of war, were slight compared to those which had
been wrought by litigation and family dissension.
The property had been for years the subject of a vexa-

tious lawsuit, which had half ruined the unsuccessful
party, and the present owner of Nettleby Tower had
not cared to take personal possession of the gloomy
pile. Perhaps Mr. Auger knew that the feeling of
the neighbourhood would be against him, as the
sympathies of all would be enlisted on the side of
the descendant of that ancient family which had for
centuries dwelt in the Tower, who had been deprived
of his birthright by the will of a proud and intem-
perate father.

The old fortress had thus been suffered to fall into
decay. Grass grew in the courtyard; the wallflower
clung to the battlements; the winter snow and the
summer rain made their way through the broken
casements, and no hand had removed the mass of
wreck which lay where a furious storm had thrown
down one of the ancient chimneys. Parties of tourists
occasionally visited the gloomy place, trod the long,
dreary corridors, and heard from a wrinkled woman
accounts of the moth-eaten tapestry, and the time-
darkened family portraits that grimly frowned from
the walls. They heard tales of the last Mr. Bardon,
the proud owner of the pile; how he had been wont
to sit long and late over his bottle, carousing with
jovial companions, till the hall resounded with their
oaths and their songs; and how, more than thirty
years back, he had disinherited his only son for
marrying a farmer's daughter. Then the old woman
would, after slowly showing the way up the worn

stone steps which led round and round till they
opened on the summit of the tower, direct her
listener's attention to a small grey speck in the wide-
spreading landscape below, and tell them that Dr.
Bardon lived there in needy circumstances, in actual
sight of the place where, if every man had his right,
he would now be dwelling as his fathers had dwelt.
And the visitors would sigh, shake their heads, and
moralize on the strange changes in human fortunes.

The old woman who showed strangers over
Nettleby Tower lived in a cottage hard by; neither
she nor any other person was ever to be found in the
old halls after the sun had set. The place had the
repute of being haunted, and was left after dark to
the sole possession of the rooks, the owls, and the
bats. I must tax the faith of my readers to believe
that the old tower *was* actually haunted; not by
the ghosts of the dead, but by the spirits of evil that
are ever moving amongst the living. I must attempt with a bold hand to draw aside the mysterious
veil which divides the invisible from the visible world,
and though I must invoke imagination to my aid, it
is imagination fluttering on the confines of truth.
Bear with me, then, while I personify the spirits of
Pride and Intemperance, and represent them as
lingering yet in the pile in which for centuries they
had borne sway over human hearts.

Standing on the battlements of the grey tower,
behold two dim, but gigantic forms, like dark clouds,

that to the eye of fancy have assumed a mortal shape. The little rock-plant that has found a cradle between the crumbling stones bends not beneath their weight,—and yet how many deep-rooted hopes have they crushed! Their unsubstantial shapes cast no shadow on the wall, and yet have darkened myriads of homes! The natural sense cannot recognise their presence; the eye beholds them not, the human ear cannot catch the low thunder of their speech; and yet there they stand, terrible *realities*,—known, like the invisible plague, by their effects upon those whom they destroy!

There is a wild light in the eyes of Intemperance, not caught from the glad sunbeams that are bathing the world in glory; it is like a red meteor playing over some deep morass, and though there is often mirth in his tone, it is such mirth as jars upon the shuddering soul like the laugh of a raving maniac! Pride is of more lofty stature than his companion, perhaps of yet darker hue, and his voice is lower and deeper. His features are stamped with the impress of all that piety abhors and conscience shrinks from, for we behold him without his veil. Human infirmity may devise soft names for cherished sins, and even invest them with a specious glory which deceives the dazzled eye; but who could endure to see in all their bare deformity those two arch soul-destroyers, Intemperance and Pride?

" Nay, it was I who wrought this ruin!" exclaimed

the former, stretching his shadowy hand over the desolated dwelling. "Think you that had Hugh Bardon possessed his senses unclouded by my spell, he would ever have driven forth from his home his own —his only son?"

"Was it not I," replied Pride, "who ever stood beside him, counting up the long line of his ancestry, inflaming his soul with legends of the past, making him look upon his own blood as something different from that which flows in the veins of ordinary mortals, till he learned to regard a union with one of lower rank as a crime beyond forgiveness?"

"I," cried Intemperance, "intoxicated his brain"—

"I," interrupted Pride, "intoxicated his spirit. You fill your deep cup with fermented beverage; the fermentation which I cause is within the soul, and it varies according to the different natures that receive it. There is the *vinous* fermentation, that which man calls high spirit, and the world hails with applause, whether it sparkle up into courage, or effervesce into hasty resentment. There is the *acid* fermentation; the sourness of a spirit brooding over wrongs and disappointments, irritated against its fellow-man, and regarding his acts with suspicion. This the world views with a kind of compassionate scorn, or perhaps tolerates as something that may occasionally correct the insipidity of social intercourse. And there is the third, the last stage of fermentation, when hating and hated of all, wrapt up in his own self-worship, and poisoning the atmosphere around with the exhalations of rebellion and unbelief, my slave becomes, even to his fellow-bondsmen, an object of aversion and disgust. Such was my power over the spirit of Hugh Bardon. I quenched the parent's yearning over his son; I kept watch even by his bed of death; and when holy words of warning were spoken, I made him turn a deaf ear to the charmer, and hardened his soul to destruction!"

"I yield this point to you," said Intemperance, "I grant that your black badge was rivetted on the miserable Bardon even more firmly than mine. And yet, what are your scattered conquests to those which I hourly achieve! Do I not drive my thousands and tens of thousands down the steep descent of folly, misery, disgrace, till they perish in the gulf of ruin? Count the gin-palaces dedicated to me in this professedly Christian land; are they not crowded with my victims? Who can boast a power to injure that is to be compared to mine?"

"Your power is great," replied Pride, "but it is a power that has limits, nay, limits that become narrower and narrower as civilization and religion gain ground. You have been driven from many a stately abode, where once Intemperance was a welcome guest, and have to cower amongst the lowest of the low, and seek your slaves amongst the vilest of the vile. Seest thou yon church," continued Pride, pointing to the spire of a small, but beautiful edifice, embowered

amongst elms and beeches ; "hast thou ever dared
so much as to touch one clod of the turf on which
falls the shadow of that building?"

"It is, as you well know, forbidden ground," replied Intemperance.

"To you—to you, but not to me!" exclaimed
Pride, his form dilating with exultation.   "I enter
it unseen with the worshippers, my voice blends with
the hymn of praise; nay, I sometimes mount the
pulpit with the preacher,* and while a rapt audience
hang upon his words, infuse my secret poison into
his soul!   When offerings are collected for the poor,
how much of the silver and the gold is tarnished and
tainted by my breath !   The very monuments raised
to the dead often bear the print of my touch ; I fix
the escutcheon, write the false epitaph, and hang my
banner boldly even over the Christian's tomb!"

"Your power also has limits," quoth Intemperance.   "There is an antidote in the inspired Book
for every poison that you can instil."

"I know it, I know it," exclaimed Pride, "and
marks it not the extent of my influence and the
depth of the deceptions that I practise, that against
no spirit, except that of Idolatry, are so many warn-
ings given in that Book as against the spirit of Pride?
For every denunciation against Intemperance, how

---

* "What a beautiful sermon you gave us to-day!" exclaimed a lady to her pastor.
"The devil told me the very same thing while I was in the pulpit," was his quaint,
but comprehensive reply.

many may be found against me! Not only religion and morality are your mortal opponents, but self-interest and self-respect unite to weaken the might of Intemperance ; *I* have but one foe that I fear, one that singles me out for conflict! As David with his sling to Goliath, so to Pride is the Spirit of the Gospel!"

"How is it, then," inquired Intemperance, "that so many believers in the Gospel fall under your sway?"

"It is because I have so many arts, such subtle devices, I can change myself into so many different shapes; I steal in so softly that I waken not the sentinel Conscience to give an alarm to the soul! *You* throw one broad net into the sea where you see a shoal within your reach ; *I* angle for my prey with skill, hiding my hook with the bait most suited to the taste of each of my victims. *You* pursue your quarry openly before man ; *I* dig the deep hidden pit-fall for mine. *You* disgust even those whom you en-slave; *I* assume forms that rather please than offend. Sometimes I am 'a pardonable weakness,' sometimes 'a natural instinct,' sometimes," and here Pride curled his lip with a mocking smile, "I am welcomed as 'a generous virtue!'"

"It is in this shape," said Intemperance angrily, "that you have sometimes even taken a part against me ! You have taught my slaves to despise and break from my yoke !"

"Pass over that," replied Pride; "or balance against

it the many times when I have done you a service, encouraging men to be *mighty to mingle strong drink*."

"Nay, you must acknowledge," said Intemperance, "that we now seldom work together."

"We have different spheres," answered Pride. "You keep multitudes from ever even attempting to enter the fold; I put my manacles upon tens of thousands who deem that they already have entered. I doubt whether there be one goodly dwelling amongst all those that dot yonder wide prospect, where one, if not all of the inmates, wears not my invisible band round the arm."

"You will except the pastor's, at least," said Intemperance. "Yonder, on the path that leads to the school, I see his gentle daughter. She has warned many against me; and with her words, her persuasions, her prayers, has driven me from more than one home. I shrink from the glance of that soft, dark eye, as if it carried the power of Ithuriel's spear. Ida seems to me to be purity itself; upon her, at least, you can have no hold."

"Were we nearer," laughed the malignant spirit, "you would see my dark badge on the saint! Since her childhood I have been striving and struggling to make Ida Aumerle my own. Sometimes she has snapped my chain, and I am ofttimes in fear that she will break away from my bondage for ever. But methinks I have a firm hold over her now."

"Her pride must be spiritual pride," observed Intemperance.

"Not so," replied his evil companion; "I tried that spell, but my efforts failed. While with sweet voice and winning persuasion Ida is now guiding her class to Truth, and warning her little flock against us both, would you wish to hearken to the story of the maiden, and hear all that I have done to win entrance into a heart which the grace of God has cleansed?"

"Tell me her history," said Intemperance; "she seems to me like the snowdrop that lifts its head above the sod, pure as a flake from the skies."

"Even the snowdrop has its roots in the earth," was the sardonic answer of Pride.

CHAPTER II.

RESISTED, YET RETURNING.

" Mount up, for heaven is won by prayer;
  Be sober— for thou art not there ! "   KEBLE.

" The sacred pages of God's own book
  Shall be the spring, the eternal brook,
  In whose holy mirror, night and day,
  Thou'lt study heaven's reflected ray.
  And should the foes of virtue dare
  With gloomy wing to seek thee there,
  Thou will see how dark their shadows lie,
  Between heaven and thee, and trembling fly."
                      MOORE.

" IDA AUMERLE," began the dark narrator, " at the
age of twelve had the misfortune to lose her mother,
and was left, with a sister several years younger
than herself, to the sole care of a tender and indulgent
father. Ever on the watch to strengthen my inte-
rests amongst the children of men, I sounded the
dispositions of the sisters, to know what chance I
possessed of making them prisoners of Pride. Mabel,
clever, impulsive, fearless in character, with a mind
ready to receive every impression, and a spirit full
of energy and emulation, I knew to be one who was
likely readily to come under the power of my spell.
Ida was less easily won ; she was a more thoughtful,
contemplative girl, her temper was less quick, her

passions were less easily roused, and I long doubted where lay the weak point of character on which Pride might successfully work.

"As Ida grew towards womanhood my doubts were gradually dispelled. I marked that the fair maiden loved to linger opposite the mirror which reflected her tall, slight, graceful form, and that the gazelle eyes rested upon it with secret satisfaction. There was much time given to braiding the hair and adorning the person; and the fashion of a dress, the tint of a ribbon, became a subject for grave consideration. There are thousands of girls enslaved by the pride of beauty with far less cause than Ida Aumerle."

"But this folly," observed Intemperance, "was likely to give you but temporary power. Beauty is merely skin-deep, and passes away like a flower!"

"But often leaves the pride of it behind," replied his companion. "There is many a wrinkled woman who can never forget that she once was fair,—nay, who seems fondly to imagine that she can never cease to be fair; and who makes herself the laughing-stock of the world by assuming in age the attire and graces of youth. It will never be thus with Ida Aumerle.

"I thought that my chain was firmly fixed upon her, when one evening I found it suddenly torn from her wrist, and trampled beneath her feet! The household at the Vicarage had retired to rest; Ida

B

had received her father's nightly blessing, and was sitting alone in her own little room. The lamplight fell upon a form and face that might have been thought to excuse some pride, but Ida's reflections at that moment had nothing in common with me. She was bending eagerly over that Book which condemns, and would destroy me,—a book which she had ofttimes perused before, but never with the earnest devotion which was then swelling her heart. Her hands were clasped, her dark eyes swimming in joyful tears, and her lips sometimes moved in prayer,—not cold, formal prayer, such as I myself might prompt, but the outpouring of a spirit overflowing with grateful love. That was the birthday of a soul! I stood gloomily apart; I dared not approach one first conscious of her immortal destiny, first communing in spirit with her God!"

"You gave up your designs, then, in despair?"

"You would have done so," answered Pride with haughtiness; "I do not despair, I only delay. I found that pride of beauty had indeed given way to a nobler, more exalting feeling. Ida had drunk at the fountain of purity, and the petty rill of personal vanity had become to her insipid and distasteful. She was putting away the childish things which amuse the frivolous soul. Ida's time was now too well filled up with a succession of pious and charitable occupations, to leave a superfluous share to the toilette. The maiden's dress became simple, because

the luxury which she now esteemed was that of
assisting the needy,   Many of her trinkets were
laid aside, not because she deemed it a sin to wear
them, but because her mind was engrossed by higher
things.   One whose first object and desire is to please
a heavenly Master by performing angels' offices
below, is hardly likely to dwell much on the consideration that her face and her figure are comely."

"Ida is, I know, reckoned a model of every
feminine virtue," said Intemperance.   "I can con-
ceive that your grand design was now to make her
think herself as perfect as all the rest of the world
thought her."

"Ay, ay ; to involve her in spiritual pride !   But
the maiden was too much on her knees, examined
her own heart too closely, tried herself by too lofty
a standard for that.   When the faintest shadow of
that temptation fell upon her, she started as though
she had seen the viper lurking under the flowers,
and cast it from her with abhorrence !   'A sinner,
a weak, helpless sinner, saved only by the mercy,
trusting only in the strength of a higher power ;'
this Ida Aumerle not only calls herself, but actually
feels herself to be.   The power of Grace in her heart
is too strong on that point for Pride."

"And yet you hope to subject her to your sway ?"

"About two years after the night which I have
mentioned," resumed Pride, "after Ida had attained
the age of eighteen, she resided for some time at

Aspendale, the home of her uncle, Augustine Aumerle."

"One of your prisoners?" inquired Intemperance.

"Of him anon," replied the dark one, "our present
subject is his niece. At his dwelling Ida met with
one who had been Augustine's college companion,
Reginald, Earl of Dashleigh. You can just discern
the towers of his mansion faint in the blue distance
yonder."

"I know it," replied Intemperance; "I fre-
quented the place in his grandfather's time. The
present earl, as I understand, is your votary rather
than mine."

"Puffed up with pride of rank," said the stern
spirit; "but pride of rank could not withstand a
stronger passion, or prevent him from laying his fortune and title at the feet of Ida Aumerle."

"An opportunity for you!" suggested Intemperance.

"A golden opportunity I deemed it. What
woman is not dazzled by a coronet? what girl is insensible to the flattering attentions of him who owns
one, even if he possess no other recommendation,
which, with Dashleigh, is far from being the case?
There was a struggle in the mind of Ida. I whispered to her of all those gilded baubles for which
numbers have eagerly bartered happiness here, and
forfeited happiness hereafter. I set before her grand
images of earthly greatness, the pomp and trappings

of state, the homage paid by the world to station.
I strove to inflame her mind with ambition. But
here Ida sought counsel of the All-wise, and she saw
through my glittering snare. The earl, though of
character unblemished in the eyes of man, and far
from indifferent to religion, is not one whom a heaven-
bound pilgrim like Ida would choose as a companion
for life. Dashleigh's spirit is too much clogged with
earth; he is too much divided in his service; he
wears too openly my chain, as if he deemed it an
ornament or distinction. Ida prayed, reflected, and
then resolved. She declined the addresses of her
uncle's guest, and returned home at once to her
father."

"The wound which she inflicted was not a deep
one," remarked Intemperance. "Dashleigh was
speedily consoled, without even seeking comfort from
me."

"I poisoned his wound," exclaimed Pride, "and
drove him to seek instant cure. Dashleigh's rejec-
tion aroused in his breast as much indignation as
grief; and I made the disappointed and irritated man
at once offer his hand to one who was not likely
to decline it, Annabella, the young cousin of Ida."

"And what said the high-souled Ida to the sudden change in the object of his devotion?"

"I breathed in her ear," answered Pride, "the
suggestion, 'He might have waited a little longer.'
I called up a flush to the maiden's cheek when she

received tidings of the hasty engagement. But still
I met with little but repulse. With maidenly reserve Ida concealed even from her own family a secret which pride might have led her to reveal, and
none more affectionately congratulated the young
countess on her engagement, than she who might
have worn the honours which now devolved upon
another."

"Ida Aumerle appears to be gifted with such a
power of resisting your influence and repelling your
temptations, that I can scarcely imagine," quoth Intemperance, "upon what you can ground your as-
surance that you hold her captive at length. Pride
of beauty, pride of conquest, pride of ambition, she
has subdued; to spiritual pride she never has yielded.
What dart remains in your quiver when so many
have swerved from the mark?"

"Or rather, have fallen blunted from the shield of
faith," gloomily interrupted Pride. "Ida's real danger began when she thought the dart too feeble to
render it needful to lift the shield against it.
Ida, on her return home, found her father on the
point of contracting a second marriage with a lady
who had been one of his principal assistants in arranging and keeping in order the machinery of his
parish. Miss Lambert, by her activity and energy,
seemed a most fitting help-meet for a pastor. She
was Aumerle's equal in fortune and birth, and not
many years his junior in age. She had been always

on good terms with his family, and the connection appeared one of the most suitable that under the circumstances could have been formed. And so it might have proved," continued Pride, "but for me!"

"Is Mrs. Aumerle, then, under your control?"

"She is somewhat proud of her good management, of her clear common sense, of her knowledge of the world," was the dark one's reply; "and this is one cause of the coldness between her and the daughters of her husband. Ida, from childhood, had been accustomed to govern her own actions and direct her own pursuits. Steady and persevering in character, she had not only pursued a course of education by herself, but had superintended that of her more impetuous sister. Since her mother's death Ida had been subject to no sensible control, for her father looked upon her as perfection, and left her a degree of freedom which to most girls might have been highly dangerous. Thus her spirit had become more independent, and her opinions more formed than is usual in those of her age. On her father's marriage Ida found herself dethroned from the position which she so long had held. She was second where she had been first,—second in the house, second in the parish, second in the affections of a parent whom she almost idolatrously loved. I saw that the moment had come for inflicting a pang; you will believe that the opportunity was not trifled

away! Ida had been accustomed to lead rather
than to follow. She exercised almost boundless influence over her sister Mabel, and was regarded as
an oracle by the poor. Another was now taking
her place, and another whose views on many subjects
materially differed from her own, who saw various
duties in a different light, and whose character disposed her to act in petty matters the part of a zealous
reformer. I marked Ida's annoyance at changes
proposed, improvements resolved on, and I silently
pushed my advantage. I have now placed Ida in
the position of an independent state, armed to resist
encroachments from, and owning no allegiance to a
powerful neighbour. There is indeed no open war;
decency, piety, and regard for the feelings of a husband and father alike forbid all approach to that;
but there is secret, ceaseless, determined opposition.
I never suffer Ida to forget that her own tastes are
more refined, her ideas more elevated than those of
her step-mother; and I will not let her perceive that
in many of the affairs of domestic life, Mrs. Aumerle,
as she had wider experience, has also clearer judgment than herself. I represent advice from a step-
mother as interference, reproof from a step-mother
as persecution, and draw Ida to seek a sphere of her
own as distinct as possible from that of the woman
whom her father has chosen for his wife."

"Doubtless you occasionally remind the fair
maid," suggested Intemperance, "that but for her

own heroic unworldliness she might have been a peeress of the realm."

"I neglect nothing," answered Pride, "that can serve to elevate the spirit of one whom I seek to enslave. I have need of caution and reserve, though hitherto I have met with success, for it is no easy task thoroughly to blind a conscience once enlightened like that of Ida. She does even now in hours of self-examination reproach herself for a feeling towards Mrs. Aumerle which almost approaches dislike. She feels that her own peace is disturbed; for the lightest breath of sin can cloud the bright mirror of such a soul. But in such hours I hover near. I draw the penitent's attention from her own faults to those of the woman she loves not, till I make her pity herself where she should blame, and account the burden which *I* have laid upon her as a cross appointed by Heaven."

"O Pride, Pride!" exclaimed Intemperance with a burst of admiration, "I am a child in artifice compared with you!"

"Rest assured that when any young mortal is disposed to look down upon one placed above her by the will of a higher power, that pride is lingering near."

"And by what name may you be known in this particular phase of your being?" inquired Intemperance.

"The pride of self-will in the language of truth; but Ida would call me *sensitiveness*," replied the dark spirit with a gloomy smile.

CHAPTER III.

SNARES.

" But what are sun and moon, and this revolving ball
  Compared with *Him* who thus supports them all;
  Whose attributes, all-infinite, transcend
  Whate'er the mind can reach, or mortal apprehend!
  Whose words drew light from chaos drear and dark,
    Whose goodness smoothes this state of toil and trouble,
  Compared with it— the sun is as a spark—
    The boundless ocean a mere empty bubble!"

HENRY ST. GEORGE TUCKER.

" THE pastor and his wife I see approaching the
church," observed Intemperance, glancing down in
the direction of the path along which advanced a
rather stout lady, with large features and high complexion, who was leaning on the arm of a tall, handsome, but rather heavily-built man, in whose mild,
dark eyes might be traced a resemblance to those of
his daughter.

" They come early," said Pride; "he, to prepare for
service; his wife, to hear the school children rehearse
the hymns appointed for the day. This was once
Ida's weekly care; she is far more qualified for the
charge than her step-mother, and the music has
suffered from the change."

" Ida showed humility, at least, in yielding up that
charge," remarked Intemperance.

"Humility," exclaimed Pride, an expression of
ineffable scorn convulsing his shadowy features as
the word was pronounced. "I should not marvel
if Ida thought so; but hear the real state of the
case. The maiden had taken extreme pains to teach
her choir a beautiful anthem, in which a trio is introduced, which she instructed three of the girls who
had the finest voices and the most perfect taste to
sing. Mrs. Aumerle, on hearing the anthem, at once
condemned it. It was time wasted, she averred, to
teach cottage-children to sing like choristers in a
cathedral; and to make a whole congregation cease
singing in order to listen to the voices of three, was
to turn the heads of the girls, and make them fancy
themselves far above the homely duties of the state
in which Providence had been pleased to place them.
There was common sense in the observations; but
Ida saw in it simply want of taste, and at my suggestion,—*at my suggestion*," repeated Pride in triumph,
"she gave up charge of the music altogether, because
she was offended at any fault having been found in
it by one who knew so little of the subject."

"Is the minister himself a good man?" inquired
Intemperance.

"Good! yes, good, if any of the worms of earth
can be called so," replied Pride, with gloomy bitterness, "for he does not regard himself as good.
Naturally weak and corrupt are the best of mortals,
prone to fall, and liable to sin, yet I succeed in per-

suading many that the gold which is intrusted to
their keeping imparts some intrinsic merit to the clay
vessel which contains it; that the cinder, glowing
bright from the fire which pervades it, is in itself a
brilliant and beautiful thing !"

"But Lawrence Aumerle was never your captive?"

"I thought once that he would be so," replied
Pride, his features darkening at the recollection of
disappointment and failure. "Aumerle had been a
singularly prosperous man—his life had appeared one
uninterrupted course of success. Easy in circumstances, cherished in his family, a favourite in society,
beloved by the poor, with a disposition easy and
tranquil, disturbed by no violent passion,—the lot of
Aumerle was one which might well render him a
subject of envy. In the pleasantness of that lot lay
its peril. Aumerle was not the first saint who in
prosperity has thought that he should never be
moved, who has been tempted to regard earthly
blessings as tokens of Heaven's peculiar favour. He
knew little of the burden and heat of the day, still
less of the strife and the struggle. Self-satisfaction
was beginning to creep over his soul, as vegetation
mantles a standing pool over which the rough winds
never sweep. 'He is mine!' I thought, 'mine
until death, and indolence and apathy shall soon add
their links to the chain forged by pride of prosperity.'
But mine was not the only eye that was watching
the Vicar of Ayrley. There is an ever-wakeful

Wisdom which ofttimes defeats my most subtle schemes, leading the blind by a way they know not, drawing back wandering souls to the orbit of duty, even as that same Wisdom hangs the round world upon nothing, and guides the stars in their courses! My chain was suddenly snapped asunder by a blow which came from a hand of love, but which, in its needful force, laid prostrate the soul which it saved. Aumerle's loved partner was smitten with sickness, smitten unto death, and the doating husband wrestled in agonizing prayer for her who was dearer to him than life. The prayer was not granted, for the wings of the saint were fledged. She escaped, like a freed bird, from the power of temptation, for ever! Her husband remained behind,—Lawrence Aumerle was an altered man. Earth had lost for him its alluring charm, and enchained his affections no more. He was softened—humbled," continued Pride, with the bitterness of one who records his own defeat, "and in another world he will reckon as the most signal mercy of his life the tempest which scattered his joys, and dashed his hopes to the ground! Let us not speak of him more," continued the fierce spirit with impatience; "his younger brother, the stately Augustine, will not shake off my yoke so lightly."

"His pride may well be personal pride," said Intemperance, following the direction of the glance of his stern companion, "if that be he who, with the rest of the congregation, is now obeying the

summons of the church bella.   Mine eyes never
rested on a more goodly man."

" *Personal* pride !" repeated the dark one with a
mocking laugh, " Augustine Aumerle is by far too
proud for that.   He would not stoop to so childish
a weakness.   No, his is the pride of intellect, the
pride of conscious genius, the pride to mortals, perhaps, the most perilous of all, which trusts its own
power to explore impenetrable mystery, and thereby
involves in a hopeless labyrinth; that seeks to sound
unfathomable depths, and may sink for ever in the
attempt."

" Is he then a sceptic ?" inquired Intemperance.

" No, not yet, *not yet,*" murmured the tempter;
" but I am leading him in the way to become one.
I am leading him as I have before led some of the
most brilliant sons of genius.   I have made them
trust their own waxen wings, rely on the strength
of their own reason, and the higher they have risen
in their flight, the deeper and darker has been their
fall."   A gleam of savage triumph, like a flash from a
dark cloud, passed over the evil spirit as he spoke.

" Who is he with the long white hair," asked
his companion, " who even now glanced up at these
old towers with an expression so stern and so sad ?"

" He who was once their heir," replied Pride.
" You see Timon Bardon, whom you and I disinherited through the power which we possessed over
his father."

" Have you not thereby lost the son?" asked Intemperance. " Would not the pride of wealth—"

He was rudely interrupted by his associate—
" Know you not that there is also a pride of poverty?"
he cried. " Have you forgotten that there is the acid
fermentation as well as the vinous? Ha! ha! my
influence is recognised over the rich and the great;
but who knows—who knows," he repeated, clenching
his shadowy hand, "in how heavy a grasp I can hold
down the poor! But I can no longer linger here,"
continued Pride; "I must mingle with yon crowd
of worshippers, even as they enter the house of
prayer. Unless I keep close at the side of each, they
may derive some benefit from the sermon, from for-
getting to criticise the preacher."

" And I," exclaimed Intemperance, " must now
away to do my work of death amongst such as never
enter a house of prayer."

And so the two evil spirits parted, each on his
own dark errand. My tale deals only with Pride, and
rather as his influence is seen in the actions and
characters of the human beings to whom the preceding conversation related, than as possessing any
distinct existence of his own. Let these three first
chapters be regarded as a preface in dialogue, ex-
plaining the design of my little volume; or as a
glimpse of the hidden clockwork which, itself unseen,
directs the movements of everyday life. Most
thankful should I be if such a glimpse could induce

my reader to look nearer at home; if, when ubi-
quitous Pride speaks to the various characters in
this tale, the reader should ask himself whether there
be not something familiar in the tone of that voice,
and with a searching glance examine whether his
own soul be clogged with no link of the tyrant's
chain,—whether he himself be not a prisoner of
Pride.

CHAPTER IV.

A GLANCE INTO THE COTTAGE.

"Where's he for honest poverty
  Wha hangs his head, and a' that,
The coward slave, we pass him by,
  We dare be poor for a' that."
                          BURNS.

THE "small grey speck" just visible from the summit of Nettleby Tower, on nearer approach expands into a stone cottage, which, excepting that it has two storeys instead of one, and can boast an iron knocker to the door, and an apology for a verandah round the window, has little that could serve to distinguish it from the dwelling of a common labourer.

We will not pause in the little garden, even to look at the bed of polyanthus in which its possessor takes great pride; we will at once enter the single sitting-room which occupies almost the whole of the ground floor, and after taking a glance at the apartment, give a little attention to its occupants.

It is evident, even on the most superficial survey, that different tastes have been concerned in the fitting up of the cottage. Most of the furniture is plain, even to coarseness; the table is of deal, and so are the chairs, but over the first a delicate cover

c

has been thrown, and the latter—to the annoyance
of the master of the house—are adorned with a
variety of tidies, which too often form themselves
into superfluous articles of dress for those who
chance to occupy the seats.   The wall is merely
white-washed, but there has been an attempt to
make it look gay, by hanging on it pale water-
colour drawings of flowers, bearing but an imperfect
resemblance to nature.   One end of the room is devoted to the arts, and bears unmistakable evidence
of the presence of woman in the dwelling.   A green
guitar-box, from which peeps a broad pink ribbon,
occupies a place in the corner, half hidden by a little
table, on which, most carefully arranged, appear
several small articles of vertu.   A tiny, round
mirror occupies the centre, attached to an ornamental
receptacle for cards; two or three miniatures in
morocco cases, diminutive cups and saucers of porcelain, and a pair of china figures which have suffered
from time, the one wanting an arm and the other a
head,—these form the chief treasures of the collection, if I except a few gaily bound books, which are
so disposed as to add to the general effect.

At this end of the room sits a lady engaged in
cutting out a tissue paper ornament for the grate ;
for though the weather is cold, no chilliness of atmosphere would be thought to justify a fire in that
room from the 1st of April to that of November.
The lady, who is the only surviving member of the

family of Timon Bardon and his late wife the
farmer's daughter, seems to have numbered between
thirty and forty years of age,—it would be difficult
to say to which date the truth inclines, for Cecilia
herself would never throw light on the subject. Miss
Bardon's complexion is sallow ; her tresses light, the
eye-lashes lighter, and the brows but faintly defined.
There is a general appearance of whity brown about
the face, which is scarcely redeemed from insipidity
by the lustre of a pair of mild, grey eyes.

But if there be a want of colour in the countenance, the same fault cannot be found in the attire,
which is not only studiously tasteful and neat, but
richer in texture, and more fashionable in style, than
might have been expected in the occupant of so poor
a cottage.   The fact is, that Cecilia Bardon's pride
and passion is dress ; it has been her weakness since
the days of her childhood, when a silly mother delighted to deck out her first-born in all the extra-
vagance of fashion.   It is this pride which makes
the struggle with poverty more severe, and which is
the source of the selfishness which occasionally sur-
prises her friends in one, on all other points, the
most kindly and considerate of women.   Cecilia
would rather go without a meal than wear cotton
gloves, and a silk dress affords her more delight than
any intellectual feast.   She had a sore struggle in
her mind whether to expend the little savings of her
allowance on a much-needed curtain to the window

to keep out draughts in winter and glare in summer,
a subscription to the village school, or a pair of
fawn-coloured kid boots, which had greatly taken
her fancy. Prudence, Charity, Vanity, contended together, but the fawn-coloured boots carried the day!
One of them is now resting on a footstool, shewing
off as neat a little foot as ever trod on a Brussels
carpet,—at least, such is the opinion of its possessor.
Grim Pride must have laughed when he framed his
fetters of such flimsy follies as these !

Opposite to Cecilia sits her father, whose appearance, as well as character, offers a strong contrast to
that of his daughter. Dr. Bardon is a man who,
though his dress be of the commonest description,
could hardly be passed in a crowd without notice.
His dark eyes flash under thick, beetling, black
brows with all the fire of youth ; and but for the
long white hair which falls almost as low as his
shoulders, and furrows on each side of the mouth,
caused by a trick of frequently drawing the corners
downwards, Timon Bardon would appear almost too
young to be the father of Cecilia. There is something leonine in the whole cast of his countenance,
something that conveys an impression that he holds
the world at bay, will shake his white mane at its
darts, and make it feel the power of his claws. The
doctor's occupation, however, at present is of the
quietest description,—he is reading an old volume ot
theology, and his mind is absorbed in his subject.

Presently a muttered "Good!" shows that he is satisfied with his author, and Bardon, after vainly searching his pockets, rises to look for a pencil to mark the passage that he approves.

He saunters up to Cecilia's show-table, and examines the ornamental card-rack attached to the tiny round mirror.

"Never find anything useful here!" he growls to himself; then, addressing his daughter, "Why don't you throw away these dirty cards, I'm sick of the very sight of them!"

Cecilia half rises in alarm, which occasions a shower of little pink paper cuttings to flutter from her knee to the floor. "O papa! don't, don't throw them away; they're the countess's wedding cards!"

Down went the corners of the lips. "Were they a duchess's," said Dr. Bardon, "there would be no reason for sticking them there for years."

"Only one year and ten months since Annabella married," timidly interposed Cecilia.

"What is it to me if it be twenty!" said the doctor, walking up and down the room as he spoke; "she's nothing to us, and we're nothing to her!"

"O papa! you used always to like Annabella."

"I liked Annabella well enough, but I don't care a straw for the countess; and if she had cared for me, she'd have managed to come four miles to see me."

"She has been abroad for some time, and—"

"And she has done with little people like us," said the doctor, drawing himself up to his full height, and looking as if he did not feel himself to be little at all. "I force my acquaintance on no one, and would not give one flower from my garden for the cards of all the peerage."

Cecilia felt the conversation unpleasant, and did not care to keep it up. She bent down, and picked up one by one the scraps of pink paper which she had scattered. Something like a sigh escaped from her lips.

Dr. Bardon was the first to speak.

"I saw Augustine Aumerle yesterday at church ; I suppose he's on a visit to his brother the vicar."

"How very, very handsome he is !" remarked Cecilia.

"You women are such fools," said the doctor, "you think of nothing but looks."

"But he's so clever too, so wonderfully clever ! They say he carried off all the honours at Cambridge."

"Much good they will do him," growled the doctor, throwing himself down on his chair; "I got honours too when I was at college, and I might better have been sowing turnips for any advantage I've had out of them. It's the fool that gets on in the world ! "

This, by the way, was a favourite axiom of

Bardon's, first adopted at the suggestion of Pride, as
being highly consolatory to one who had never
managed to get on in the world.

"I think that I see Ida and Mabel Aumerle crossing the road," said Cecilia, glancing out of the window. "How beautiful Ida is, and so charming ! I
declare I think she's an angel ! "

"She's well enough," replied the doctor, in a tone
which said that she was that, but nothing more.

In a short time a little tap was heard at the door,
and the vicar's daughters were admitted. Ida indeed looked lovely ; a rapid walk in a cold wind
had brought a brilliant rose to her cheek, and as
she laid on the table a large paper parcel which she
and her sister had carried by turns, her eyes beamed
with benevolent pleasure. Mabel was far less attractive in appearance than her sister, a small upturned nose robbing her face of all pretensions to
beauty beyond what youth and good-humour might
give; but she also looked bright and happy, for the
girl's errand was one of kindness. The want of a
curtain in Bardon's cold room had been noticed by
others than Cecilia, and the parcel contained a crimson one made up by the young ladies themselves.

"Oh ! what a beauty! what a love!" exclaimed
Cecilia, in the enthusiasm of grateful admiration.
"Papa, only see what a splendid curtain dear Ida
and Mabel have brought us !"

The doctor was not half so enthusiastic. It has

been said that there are four arts difficult of attain-
ment,—*how to give reproof, how to take reproof, how
to give a present, and how to receive one.* This
difficulty is chiefly owing to pride. Timon Bardon
was more annoyed at a want having been perceived,
than gratified at its having been removed. He
would gladly enough have obliged the daughters of
his pastor, but to be under even a small obligation
to them was a burden to his sensitive spirit. He
could hardly thank his young friends ; and a stranger
might have judged from his manner that the
Aumerles were depriving him of something that he
valued, rather than adding to his comforts. But
Ida knew Bardon's character well, and made allowance for the temper of a peevish, disappointed man.
She seated herself by Cecilia, and began at once on a
different topic.

"I have a message for you, Miss Bardon. I saw
Annabella on Saturday."

"The countess ! " cried the expectant Cecilia.

"She was at our house, and regretted that the
threatening weather prevented her driving on here."

"I'd have been so delighted ! " interrupted
Cecilia, while the doctor muttered to himself some
inaudible remark.

"But she desired me to say, with her love, how
much pleasure it would give her if you and her old
friend the doctor (these were her words) would
come to see her at Dashleigh Hall."

The grey eyes of Miss Bardon lighted up with irrepressible pleasure, and even the gruff old doctor uttered a rather complacent grunt.

"She begged," said Mabel, "that you would drive over some morning and take luncheon, and let her show you over the garden and park."

"Then she's not changed, dear creature!" exclaimed Cecilia.

"And she hopes before long," continued Mabel, "to find herself again at Milton Cottage."

"Mill Cottage," said the doctor gruffly; for the name of his tenement had for many years been a disputed subject between him and his daughter Cecilia;—"there's common sense in that name: Mill Cottage, because it was once connected with a mill. To turn it into 'Milton' is pure nonsense and affectation. A fine title would hang about as well on this place as knee-buckles and ruff on a ploughman!" And having thus given his oracular opinion, Dr. Bardon strolled out into his garden, leaving the young ladies to pursue uninterrupted conversation together, none the less agreeable for his absence.

"You will excuse papa," said Cecilia, feeling that some apology was required for her father's abrupt departure.

Dr. Bardon's manner was far rougher and less courteous than it would have been had he appeared as the lord of Nettleby Tower, instead of a poor

surgeon with indifferent practice. Whether it were
that he was soured by disappointment, or that his
pride shrank from the idea of appearing to cringe to
those more favoured by fortune than himself, it
would be perhaps difficult to determine ; he appeared
to consider that true dignity consisted in despising
these outward advantages which he would probably
have overvalued had he himself possessed them.
Thus, while Cecilia's pride led her to make the best
possible appearance, and catch any reflected gleam
of grandeur from opulent or titled acquaintance, Dr.
Bardon rather gloried in the meanness of his home,
never cared to hide the patch upon his coat, and
considered himself equal in his poverty to any peer
who wore the garter and the George.

The doctor appeared to have walked off his ill-
humour, for when Ida and Mabel bade adieu to Miss
Bardon, they found him ready to escort them to his
gate. With not ungraceful courtesy he presented
the young ladies with a nosegay of his choicest
hyacinths, and even condescended to say that he
valued their present for the sake of the fair hands
that had worked it ! There was something of the
"fine old English gentleman" lingering yet about
the disinherited man.

CHAPTER V

BOTH SIDES.

"From idle words, that restless throng
    And haunt our hearts when we would pray ;
From pride's false chain, and jarring wrong,
    Seal Thou my lips, and guard the way."

KEBLE.

"Now the doctor's happy! he has ·got rid of his gratitude! I knew how it would be!" laughed Mabel, as soon as the girls had walked beyond reach of hearing.

"What do you mean?" asked Ida.

"Did you not see how uncomfortable the poor man was under the weight of even such a little obligation? It was steam high pressure with him, till he opened a safety-valve, and off flew all his debt discharged in the shape of a bunch of hyacinths!"

"How you talk!" said her sister with a smile; "he intended these poor little flowers as a mark of attention; they were no return for our present."

"O Ida, how little you know! Why, Dr. Bardon does not think that there are hyacinths in the world that can bear comparison with his. He thinks them worth any money. He carries

a mental glass of very singular construction, patented
by the maker, Pride.   Look through the one end,
everything is small ; look through the other, everything is big !   He turns the magnifier to what he
does himself, the diminisher to what others do for
him ; and it is wonderful how he thus manages to
economize gratitude, and keep himself out of debt to
his friends.   Depend upon it, seen through his glass,
his hyacinths swelled to the size of hollyhocks,
and our curtain diminished to that of a sampler ! "

"You are a sad satirical girl ! " said Ida.

" Not I, I've only practised the ' vigilance of
observation and accuracy of distinction, which neither
books nor precepts can teach,' which the famous Mr.
Jenkins used to recommend to papa when he was
young.   I am merely distinguishing between the
kindnesses which a man does to please a friend, and
those which he does to gratify his own pride.   Dr.
Bardon, in spite of his poverty, is as proud as the
Earl of Dashleigh can be."

" But he is one who deserves much indulgence."

" I am not saying anything against him," interrupted Mabel ; "I rather like a dash of pride in
a character ; I know I have plenty of it myself."

" Mabel—"

" Why, darling, I'm proud of you ! " exclaimed
Mabel, turning her eyes affectionately on her sister ;
" and I'm proud of my excellent father, proud of my
glorious uncle, but I am not proud,"—here Mabel

laughed,—" I'm not proud of my step-mother at all."

" Mabel, dearest— "

" I'm convinced that the world may be divided into two classes—those made of porcelain, and those of crockery. There seems such a wonderful difference in the nature of minds, into whatever shape education may twist them ! Now, my father, uncle, and you, are made of real Sevres porcelain, and Mrs. Aumerle—"

" Really, Mabel, you do wrong to speak thus of her."

" Well, I won't if you don't like it, darling, but she's so intensely common-place and matter-of-fact ! I don't believe that she understands or could enter into our feelings any more than if we had been born in different planets ! "

Ida sighed. " It is our appointed trial," she replied ; and these few words, though well intended, did more to impress upon her young sister the hardship of having an uncongenial stepmother, than open complaint might have done. Mabel regarded her gentle sister as a suffering saint, and had no idea that there might be two sides even to such a question as this.

Ida's conscience warned her that the preceding conversation had been unprofitable, to say the least of it, and she knew well what Scripture saith against *every idle word.* She therefore turned the channel of discourse, and told Mabel of her new plan of having a class for farm-boys, which she intended herself to conduct.

"You can't manage more upon Sundays, Ida; you have two classes already, you know."

"True; this must be on the Saturday evening, when the lads have left off work."

"You can't have the school-room, then; that's Mrs. Aumerle's time for the mother's class."

"I have been thinking about that," said Ida, gravely; "but there is really no other hour that will be suitable at all for mine. I must ask Mrs. Aumerle to have her women a little earlier in the afternoon."

"I would not ask a favour of her!" said Mabel proudly.

"It is never pleasant to ask favours," replied Ida; "but it is sometimes our duty to do so."

It was growing dark before the sisters reached their home. They found Mrs. Aumerle busily engaged in cutting out clothes for the poor, wielding her large, bright scissors with quick hand, and directing its operations with an experienced eye. She looked up from her occupation as Ida and Mabel entered the room.

"What has made you so late?" asked the lady.

"Oh! we have had a nice, long chat with Cecily Bardon," replied Mabel; "we never thought of the hour."

" I hope that you will think of it another time,"
said Mrs. Aumerle, resuming her cutting and clipping;
" it is not proper for young ladies to be crossing the
fields after sunset without an escort."

" Not proper!" repeated Mabel half aloud, her
cheek suffused with an angry flush.

" We have been always accustomed," said Ida
more calmly, " to walk whither and at what hour we
pleased, and we have never found the smallest inconvenience arise from so doing."

" Your having done so is no reason why you
should do so," said the lady firmly; " you have been
too much left to yourselves, and it is well that you
have now some one of a little experience to judge
what is suitable or unsuitable for two young girls of
your age."

Mabel turned down the corners of her mouth after
the fashion of Dr. Bardon; happily Mrs. Aumerle
was too busy with a jacket-sleeve to look at her step-
daughter's face. Ida seated herself without reply;
but Pride stole up at that moment and whispered in
her ear, " You can manage quite as well for yourself
as the meddling dame can manage for you. She
might be content to let well alone, and confine herself to her own affairs."

Ida now entered upon the subject of the class for
farmers' boys and labouring lads, and explained the
necessity for holding it on the particular day and
hour on which the mothers' meeting usually took

place. She dwelt with gentle eloquence upon the
difficulties and temptations of the youths who would
be benefited by the new arrangement ; but it tried
her patience not a little to hear the snip-snip of the
scissors all the time that she was speaking.

" Well, I'll consider the matter," said Mrs. Aumerle,
stopping at length in her occupation ; " it will cause
me a little inconvenience, but I think that the thing
may be managed.   But," she continued, as Ida,
having gained her point, was about to leave the
apartment, " but we have not thought of the most
important thing—who is to conduct the class?"

" I had thought of it," replied Ida ; " I am going
to conduct it myself."

" You !" exclaimed Mrs. Aumerle, turning towards
Ida a face whose naturally high colour was heightened
by stooping over her cutting ; " you ! the thing is
not to be dreamed of !   Your father's daughter to be
teaching and preaching to a set of hulking farm lads,
as if they were a parcel of little schoolboys!   It
would not become a young lady like you."

" I have yet to learn what can become a lady, be
she old or young, better than teaching the ignorant
and helping the poor," said Ida with forced calmness,
but great constraint and coldness of manner.

" Oh ! that's very fine talking, my dear ; the
thing may be a very good thing in itself, but we
must choose different instruments for different kinds
of work.   One would not mend quills with scissors,

or cut out flannel with a pen-knife. I can't hear of your holding such a class."

Commanding herself sufficiently not to reply, but with an angry and swelling heart Ida sought her own room, followed by the indignant Mabel. No sooner had they reached it than Mabel threw her arms around Ida, and exclaimed, " My own darling, angel sister ! how dared she speak so to you!"

" She will grieve one day," said Ida, struggling to keep down tears, " that she has put any stumbling-block in the way of such a work. Mabel, we must pity and pray for her !"

" And never let yourselves be led by her," suggested Pride.

" That girl wants somebody to guide her;" such were the reflections of Mrs. Aumerle, as she went on with her work for the poor. "There's a great deal of good in her, but she wants ballast,—she wants common-sense. She is spoilt by being so long without the control of a mother, and needs, almost as much as saucy Mabel, a good firm hand over her. With all Ida's gentleness and meekness, there's in her a world of obstinacy and pride. I wish that I had brought one verse to her recollection, which she seems to leave out when she reads the Bible— *Likewise ye younger, submit yourselves unto the elder ; yea, all of you be subject one to another, and be clothed with humility ; for God resisteth the proud, and giveth grace to the humble.* Ida has a wonder-

D

ful conceit of her own opinion, as most inexperienced
young people have ; and it's almost impossible to
convince her that she ever can be wrong.   She is not
wrong, however, about the duty of having a class for
these poor farm lads ; I must consult Lawrence as to
how it can be done." The lady went on with her
cogitations upon the subject. "We could not expect
our schoolmaster to undertake such an addition to
his labours. The clerk, Ashby—no, no, he's not fitted
for it ; he'd set the young fellows yawning,—no one
would come twice for his teaching. Perhaps the
best plan would be for me to take the lads myself,
and give up my mother's meeting to Ida. It would
be far more suitable for a pretty young creature like
her.   But I must keep the cutting out and shaping
of the poor-clothes still, for clever as she is in reading and talking, that is a business which poor Ida
never could manage with all the goodwill in the
world."

And so the plain, practical stepmother settled the
matter in her own mind ; and only Pride could suggest that her plan was inconvenient, inconsiderate,
or unkind.   It was ultimately adopted by Ida, but
with a reluctance and coldness which deprived both
ladies of the encouragement and pleasure which they
would have derived from cheerful, hearty, co-opera-
tion with each other in labours of love.

CHAPTER VI.

THE VISIT TO THE HALL.

"The tulip and the butterfly
Appear in gayer coats than I;
Let me be dressed fine as I will,
Flies, flowers, and worms excel me still."   WATTS.

THE visit of the sisters Aumerle, or rather the message which they had brought, had caused great excitement in the mind of Cecilia Bardon. One thought was now uppermost there, thrusting itself forward at all times, interfering with domestic duties, taking her attention even from her prayers; that thought was—how should she persuade her father to pay a visit to Dashleigh Hall!

Dr. Bardon held out against entreaties for two days; on the third he yielded, having probably all along only made show of fight to avoid seeming eagerly to catch at an invitation from a titled acquaintance.

The next question was—How was the visit to be paid? Four miles was a distance too great to be traversed on foot by Cecilia Bardon.

"We could get a neat clarence from Pelton," suggested the lady.

"Pelton!" exclaimed the doctor,—"why, Pelton is six miles off! You'll not find me paying for a clarence to go twenty miles to carry me to a place to which I could walk any fine morning. I've not money to fling away after that fashion."

"If only the Aumerles kept a carriage!" sighed Cecilia.

"If they kept fifty I'd not ask for the loan of one," said the doctor, with all the pride of poverty.

"Dear me! how shall we ever get to Dashleigh Hall!" cried Cecilia.

"I'll tell you what, I'll hire our neighbour the farmer's donkey-chaise,—that won't ruin even a poor man like me."

"A donkey-chaise!" exclaimed Miss Bardon in horror.

"Why, you've been glad enough of it before now to carry you over to Pelton, when you had shopping to do in the town."

"Pelton,—why, yes,—shopping,—but to call on a countess!"

"A countess, I suppose, is made of flesh and blood like other people; if she's such an idiot as to care whether her friends come to her in chariots or donkey-chaises, the less we have to do with her the better, say I."

"But to drive through the park—to go up to the grand hall, to—to—to be seen by all the fine liveried servants—"

The doctor actually stamped with impatience. "What is it to us," he cried, "if all the lackeys in Christendom were to see us? We're doing nothing wrong—nothing to be ashamed of. I should be as much a gentleman in a chaise, or a cart, drawn by a donkey or a dog, as if I'd fifty racers in my stables, and a handle a mile long to my name."

The pride of the father and the daughter were at variance, but it was the same passion that worked in both. Cecilia sought dignity in accessories, Dr. Bardon found it in self. She would climb up to distinction in the world by grasping at every advantage held out by the rank and wealth of her friends; he would rise also, but by trampling under foot rank and wealth as things to be despised. The pride of the daughter was most ridiculous—that of the father most deadly. Reader, do you know nothing of either?

One of the things on which Bardon prided himself was on being master in his own house—no very difficult matter, as his subjects consisted but of one gentle-tempered daughter, and one old deaf domestic. On the present occasion Cecilia soon found that she must go to Dashleigh Hall in a donkey-carriage, if she intended to go at all; and after a longer struggle than usual, which ended in something like tears, she yielded to the pressure of circumstances, and consented to accompany her father the next day in the ignoble vehicle which he had selected. This point settled, her mind was free to give itself to the

darling subject of dress. Half the day was devoted
to touching and retouching last summer's bonnet,
which looked rather the worse for wear, and selecting such articles of attire as might give a distinguished and fashionable air to the lady of Milton Cottage. Cecilia was not unsuccessful. Never,
perhaps, had a more elegantly dressed woman
stepped into a donkey-chaise before. Her flounced
silk dress expanded to such fashionable dimensions as
scarcely to leave space in the humble conveyance for
the accommodation of the doctor.

If her dress was an object of triumph to Miss Bardon, it was also one of solicitude and care. Never,
surely, were roads so dusty, and never was dust more
annoying. Her nervous anxiety and precautions
irritated the temper of the doctor, who found more
than enough to try it in the obstinacy of the animal
that he drove, without further provocation from his
companion. Both father and daughter were well
pleased when they at length reached the ornamental
lodge of Dashleigh Park.

"Papa," suggested Cecilia timidly, "could we not
leave the donkey to graze in the lane, and go through
the grounds on foot?"

"Leave the hired donkey to be carried off by any
party of tramping gipsies! I'm not such a fool," said
the doctor.

The lodge-keeper obeyed the summons of the bell,
which was rung with more force than was needful;

he stood still, however, without opening the gate, to
inquire what the occupants of the donkey-chaise
wanted.

"Open the gate, will you?" cried the doctor, in
his rough, domineering manner.

"For Dr. and Miss Bardon, of Milton Cottage,
friends of the countess," said Cecilia nervously, feeling very uncomfortable at her own position.

The gate-keeper looked hesitatingly at the lady,
then at the chaise, then at the lady again. It is
possible that her appearance decided his doubts, or
that the impatience of the doctor overbore them, for
the gate slowly rolled back on its hinges, and the
donkey-chaise entered the park.

Cecilia could scarcely find any charm in the beautiful drive, magnificent timber, verdant glades, broad
avenues affording glimpses of distant prospects, sunny
knolls on which grazed the light-footed deer. She
could not, however, refrain from an exclamation of
delight as a sudden bend in the road brought her unexpectedly in sight of the lordly Hall.

Dr. Bardon surveyed the splendid building before
him with a gloomy, dissatisfied eye. What was it
compared to Nettleby Tower, in the mind of the disinherited man? "Mere gingerbread! mere gingerbread!" he muttered to himself, as he drew up at the
lofty entrance. He saw more beauty in a ruined but-
tress of the ancient home of his fathers than in all the
florid decorations of the countess's magnificent abode.

Cecilia Bardon was well-nigh overpowered by the
sense of the grandeur before her.   The presence of
three or four of the earl's powdered footmen was
enough in itself to make her seat in the donkey-
chaise almost intolerable to the lady.

"Lady Dashleigh at home?" inquired the doctor
from his low seat, in a tone that would have sounded
haughty from a prince.

The countess was happily at home ; and Cecilia,
hastily descending, breathed more freely when no
longer in contact with the odious conveyance.   She
felt something as a prisoner may feel when he has
left the jail behind, his connection with which he
desires to forget, wishing that all others could do
so likewise.   Dr. Bardon flung the rein on the neck of
the donkey, and followed his daughter into the Hall.

They were introduced into a splendid apartment,
fitted up with magnificence and taste.   Poor Cecilia,
as she there awaited the countess, painfully con-
trasted the room with its glittering mirrors and
gilded ceiling, painted panels and velvet cushions,
with the homeliness of her own humble abode.
Pride, who revels in human misery, would not
omit the opportunity of inflicting an envious pang.
But his barbed dart went deeper—far deeper into
the heart of the unhappy Bardon—the man who
would have scornfully laughed at the idea of the
possibility of such as he envying any mortal in the
world.

Cecilia had scarcely time to gaze around her, shake out her dusty flounces, and glance in a mirror to see if her scarf fell gracefully, when Annabella herself appeared from an inner apartment.

The appearance of the youthful countess was rather attractive than striking. Her figure was below the middle height, and so light and delicate in its proportions as to have earned for Annabella in girlhood the title of Titania, queen of the fairies. Her complexion had not the purity of that of her cousin Ida; but any emotion or excitement suffused her cheek with a beautiful crimson, and lit up the vivacious dark eyes, which were the only decidedly pretty feature in a face whose chief charm lay in its ever-varying expression. The irregular outline of the countess's profile deprived her countenance of all claim to absolute beauty, but no one when under the spell of her winning conversation, could pause to criticise or even notice defects where the general effect was so pleasing. The dress of the countess was not such as might have been expected in one of her rank. It was picturesque rather than costly, fanciful rather than fashionable. Annabella had just been bending over her desk, busy with a romance which she was writing; her tresses were slightly disordered, and a small ink stain actually soiled the whiteness of one little delicate finger.

Her greeting to Dr. and Miss Bardon was most gracious and cordial. She came forward with both

hands extended, and welcomed her old friends to
Dashleigh Hall with a frank kindliness which at once
set Cecilia at her ease. "She is not changed in the
least ; she is the same fascinating being as ever," was
the reflection of the gratified guest.

Dr. Bardon was not so easily won. He was out
of temper with himself and all the world. The touch
of pride had turned indeed his wine of life into a
concentrated acid. Annabella could not but notice
the hardness of his manner, but she was neither surprised nor offended, for she knew the character of
the man. "I will conquer the old lion ! " thought
she, and she exerted all her powers to do so. How
thoughtfully attentive the countess became, how she
humoured her guest's little fancies, how she avoided
jarring upon his prejudices, and talked of old times,
old scenes, old friends, till she fairly beat down, one
after another, every barrier behind which ill-humour
could lurk !

Annabella took the arm of the doctor, and with
Cecilia at her side, sauntered down the marble ter-
race into the garden. She consulted Timon Bardon
about the disposition of her flower-beds, asked advice
concerning the management of plants, and finally
overcame the old lion altogether by begging for a
slip from his Venice Sumach. The moment that
the doctor found that he could confer a favour instead of accepting one, all his equanimity returned;
and when the party re-entered the beautiful drawing-

room, the only shadow on the enjoyment of any of the three was Cecilia's consciousness that the gravel-walks had impaired the beauty of her fawn-coloured boots.

"What a sweet creature the countess is!" was Miss Bardon's silent reflection; "prosperity has done her no harm; she has not a particle of pride!"

CHAPTER VII.

A MISADVENTURE.

"Where pride and passion frame the nuptial chain,
  Time must the gilding from the fetter wear;
Love's golden links alone unchanged remain,
  Hallowed by faith, to be renewed in heaven again."

"SHE has not a particle of pride!" Such may be
the judgment of the world, which looks not below
the surface, but the recording angel may give a
very different account. Let us examine a little more
closely into the character of the countess, and see if
she may fairly be ranked amongst the *poor in spirit*,
of whom is the *kingdom of heaven.*

Annabella had been an orphan almost from her
birth, and had been brought up by a tender grand-
mother, since deceased, who had made an idol of her
little darling, the heiress to all her wealth. As soon
as the child had power to frame a sentence, that sentence was law to the household. Annabella, the
fairy queen, acquired a habit of ruling, which gave a
permanent cast to her mind. Gifted with joyous
spirits, a sweet temper, and a strong desire to please,
her pride was seldom offensive. Annabella's subjects
were willing, for the sovereign was beloved.

As the child grew into the woman, her views began to expand; she desired a wider sway. Annabella was not contented to rule merely in a household, to influence only a small circle of friends. Like those who cut their names on a pyramid, she was ambitious of leaving her mark on the world. The only instrument by which it seemed possible to accomplish this object of ambition was the pen. If "the press" is the fourth power in the state, Annabella resolved to have a share in that power. She had a lively fancy, a ready wit, and, to her transporting delight, her first essay was successful. The young lady's contributions to a monthly periodical were indeed sent under a *nom de guerre*, but Annabella's darling hope was to make that adopted title of "Egeria" famous throughout the land.

It was at this point of her history that the Earl of Dashleigh, smarting under the sting of mortified pride, and casually thrown much into the charming society of Annabella, made her the offer of his hand. The eye of the young heiress had not, like that of her cousin Ida, been fixed upon objects so high that the glare of earthly grandeur died away before it like the sparkles of fireworks below. Annabella was completely dazzled by the idea of such a brilliant alliance. Her imagination immediately invested the young earl with every great and glorious quality. Love threw a halo around him, and the maiden fancied that she saw realized in her noble suitor every

poetical dream of her girlhood. Nor was love the
only chord that vibrated to rapture in the heart of
Dashleigh's young bride. Did not this elevation to
rank and dignity offer at once a wider sphere to her
eager ambition? From the rapidity of her conquest,
Annabella deemed that her power over the earl
would be unbounded, little imagining how much that
conquest was owing to the effect of his pride and
pique.

Marriage soon undeceived Annabella. She found
herself united to a man at least as proud as herself,
though his pride took a different form. As long as
the bride was contented simply to please, there was
domestic harmony; Annabella was happy in her
husband, and he thought that no companion could be
so agreeable as his witty and lively wife. But the
moment that the countess attempted to rule, the
elements of discord began to work. The earl, who
never lost consciousness of high birth and distinguished rank, was aware that he had married one
who, though of good family, was yet considerably
below himself in social position. This, however,
would have mattered little, had Annabella readily
accommodated herself to the new circumstances in
which she was placed. The nobleman, in the famous
old tale, had deigned to wed even the humble Griselda; he had had no reason to regret his choice, but
then there was a difference, wide as north from south,
between Griselda and Annabella! As soon as the

young countess became aware that her husband felt
that he had stooped a little when he raised her to
share his rank, all her pride at once rose in arms.
She was more determined than ever to assert the
independence which she regarded as the right of her
sex.

The bond which pride had first helped to form
was ill fitted to bear the daily strain which was now
put upon it. Annabella, all the romance of courtship over, saw her idol without its gilding, the halo
of fancy faded away, and he over whom its lustre had
been thrown, appeared but as an ordinary mortal.
In a thousand little ways, scarcely apparent to any
but the parties immediately concerned, the habits
and wishes of the ill-assorted couple jarred painfully
on each other. Pride revelled in his work of mischief as he glided from the one to the other.

" Your wife," he would whisper to the earl, " with
all her talents, and all her charms, is ill fitted for the
station which she holds. She has not the dignity,
the stateliness of mien which would beseem the lady
of Dashleigh Hall. She has vulgar tastes, vulgar
friends, vulgar amusements. Her very dress is not
such as becomes the wife of a peer of the realm. She
is giddy, fantastic, and vain, and altogether devoid
of a due sense of your condescension in placing her
at the head of your splendid establishment. Your
choice has been a mistake."

Then the spirit of mischief would breathe out his

treason to Annabella : "Your husband, if superior
to you in descent, you have now discovered to be so
in no single other point. He has neither your wit
nor your spirit. He is rather a weak, though an
obstinate man, and thinks much more than common-
sense warrants of what has been called 'the accident
of birth.' Have you not much more reason to exult
in belonging to the aristocracy of talent, than that of
mere rank like him ? Do you glory in the name of
Countess as you do in that of 'Egeria,' by which
alone you are known to reading thousands ?"

Having thus given my readers a glimpse of "the
skeleton in the house" where all appears outwardly
so full of enjoyment, I will take up my thread where
I laid it down, and return to the drawing-room of
Dashleigh Hall.

Dr. Bardon, as we have seen, had been restored to
good humour by the tact and attentions of the countess, and Cecilia exhausted all her superlatives in
admiration of everything that she saw. The conversation flowed pleasantly between Annabella and
the doctor, for Bardon was a well read and intelli-
gent man, and literature was the countess's passion.
Cecilia, however, found the discourse assuming too
much of the character of a *tête-à-tête*, and not being
content to remain exclusively a listener, watched
eagerly for an opportunity to drop in her little contri-
bution to "the feast of reason and the flow of soul."

"Yes, the world is much like a library," said

Annabella, in reply to an observation from the doctor, "but most persons enter it rather to give a superficial glance at the binding of the books, than to make themselves masters of the contents."

"They are satisfied if the gilding lie thick enough on the backs of the tomes," said the doctor.

"But what a deep, what a curious study would every character be, if we could read it through from beginning to end (skipping the preface, of course, for school-boys and school-girls are objects of natural aversion). What romances would some lives disclose —while others would offer the most forcible sermons that ever were written. What exquisite beauty, what touching poetry we might find in the daily course of some whom now we regard with little attention!"

"Your lovely Cousin Ida, for instance," chimed in Cecilia, trying to catch the tone of the conversation, "I always think of her as a living poem!"

"If Ida be a poem," said Annabella rather coldly, "she is certainly one in blank verse,—a new version of 'Young's Night Thoughts,' exceedingly admirable and sublime!"

The countess had always professed herself attached to her cousin, with whom she had from childhood interchanged a thousand little tokens of affection. She would have done much to promote the happiness of Ida, or to avert from her any real sorrow, and yet —strange contradiction—Annabella never liked to

E

hear warm praise of her friend. It almost appeared
as though the countess considered the admiration
accorded to her beautiful cousin as so much sub-
tracted from herself. When just commendation of
another excites an uneasy sensation in our minds, we
need no supernatural power to recognise in it the
fretting jar of the jealous chain which pride has fixed
on our souls.

Annabella was also at this time a little displeased
with her cousin. Ida Aumerle, from motives of
delicacy which the reader will understand though
the countess could not, had declined repeated invita-
tions to pay a long visit to Dashleigh Hall. Annabella, who was eager to show her new possessions to
the friend of her youth, was hurt at what appeared
to her to be coldness, if not unkindness. To be
easily offended is one of the most indubitable marks of
pride, and from this Annabella was certainly not free.

While the preceding conversation was proceeding
in the drawing-room, a horseman, attended by a
groom, rode up to the entrance of Dashleigh Hall.
He was a man who had scarcely yet reached the
meridian of life. His figure was graceful, though
affording small promise of physical strength; his
features well-formed, and of almost feminine delicacy,
though the prevailing expression which sat upon
them was one of conscious superiority,—now softening into condescension, now, at any real or imagined
affront, rising into that of offended dignity.

Reginald, Earl of Dashleigh—for this was he—seemed, figuratively speaking, never to be out of the cumbersome robes in which, on state occasions, he appeared as a peer of the realm. Whether he mingled in society, or conversed alone with his wife, proffered hospitality, or received it, he appeared to feel the weight of a coronet always encircling his brow. The question which he asked himself before entering upon any line of action, was less whether it were right or wrong, prudent or foolish, as whether it were worthy of Reginald, twelfth Earl of Dashleigh. Pride had kept the young nobleman from many of the vices and follies of his age ; pride had prevented him from doing anything that might injure his character in the eyes of the world, and had led him to do many things which gained for him popular applause ; but pride, at the best, is but a miserable substitute for a higher principle of action ; its fruits may appear fair to the eye, but are dust and corruption within.

The earl was not a remarkably skilful rider. Nature had not gifted him with either muscular strength or iron nerve. At the moment that he reached his own door his horsemanship was put to unpleasant proof. An incident, ludicrous as that which Cowper has celebrated in his humorous poem, proved that the same mishaps may overtake a peer of the realm, and "a citizen of credit and renown." The sudden, prolonged bray of a donkey—most unwonted sound in that lordly place—startled the steed which was ridden by the earl. Its sudden plunge unseated its rider, and the illustrious aristocrat measured his length upon the road! The accident was of no serious nature; the nobleman was in an instant again on his feet, shaking the dust from his garments; nothing had suffered from the fall but Reginald's dignity, and, consequently, his temper. The accident appeared absurd from its cause, and Dashleigh was more provoked at the occurrence than he might have been had some grave evil befallen him.

"How came that brute there?" he exclaimed to the servants, who officiously crowded around him with proffers of assistance, which were impatiently rejected by their master. "How came that brute there?" he angrily repeated, looking indignantly at the animal which had drawn Dr. Bardon's humble conveyance, and which was now quietly feeding in the luxuriant pasture of the park.

"Please you, my lord, visitors to see her ladyship came in that chaise," replied a footman, scarcely able to suppress a smile.

"Visitors!" said the earl sharply; "the milliner or the dressmaker, I suppose. Tell Mills at the lodge never again to suffer such a thing to enter the gate;" and without troubling himself with further investigation, the nobleman entered into his house. As he did so, he turned to his butler—" Let covers

be laid for three," he said, in a tone of command;
"and give the housekeeper notice that the Duke of
Montleroy is likely to be here at luncheon."

"Covers are laid already for four, by her ladyship's order," said the butler.

"Indeed! what guests are expected?" asked the
earl.

"The lady and gentleman, my lord, who came in
the chaise, and who are now in the drawing-room,"
was the reply.

The earl stalked into the library in a state, not
only of high irritation and annoyance, but also of
considerable perplexity. Annabella had never before
appeared to him so utterly regardless of his wishes
and feelings, so completely destitute of a sense of
what was due to her position. To invite low
people—for such, he thought, that her guests assuredly must be—to share her meal, to be introduced to her husband, it was an offence scarcely to
be forgiven! And what was to be done on the
present occasion? Dashleigh had, on that morning,
casually met and invited a duke! It would be impossible to insult a man of his quality by making
him sit at the same table with such *canaille!* The
idea of such a breach of etiquette was abhorrent to
the feelings of the aristocrat, and yet, how was the
reality to be avoided? Annabella had invited her
own friends, and the earl was too much of a gentleman to be willing to commit any decided breach of

couitesy towards his wife's guests, even though they
might have come in a donkey conveyance.

We talk of the *petty* miseries of pride ; to Dashleigh the misery was not petty.   It was with feelings
of serious annoyance that he rang his library bell,
and bade the servant who answered it request his ·
lady to speak with the earl directly.

The message was carried to Annabella while she
was pursuing with the doctor a playful argument on
some literary question.

" Is the earl aware that I am engaged with guests?"
asked the incautious countess.

" His lordship knows who is here," replied the
servant.

Annabella instantly perceived her mistake, for she
saw the blood mount to the cheek of the sensitive
old Doctor. His pride was evidently on the *qui vive;*
and it served to awaken hers.   The countess felt
somewhat disposed to return to her liege lord such
an answer as Horatio received from his widow.   She
had no inclination to play Griselda in the presence of
her early friends. She contented herself, however,
with showing that she was in no haste to obey the
summons of her titled husband, and finished her discussion before (after apologizing to the Bardons for
a brief absence) she proceeded to the library, where
her indignant lord was impatiently awaiting her.

Dr. Bardon walked up to the window with his
hands behind him, and waited for a space in silence.

Cecilia saw by the motion of his feet that a storm was brewing in the air. Presently he turned suddenly round with the question: " Do you suppose that this earl means to make his appearance ?"

" Ye-e-es," replied Cecilia timidly.

" No !" exclaimed the doctor fiercely. The two words, and the manner of pronouncing them, were characteristic of father and daughter, and might almost have been adopted as mottoes by the twain. " Yes" was very often on Cecilia's lips, but she appeared to feel the affirmation too short to answer the full purpose of politeness, and always managed to drawl out the monosyllable to the length of three. Bardon's " No," on the contrary, came out short and sharp, like a bark. He seemed to concentrate into it his haughty spirit of perpetual dissent from the opinions of the rest of the world.

" I should not wonder if the poor girl has got into a scrape for inviting us," was the doctor's next observation.

" Oh ! dear papa !" exclaimed Cecilia, in an expostulatory tone, though the same thought had just been passing through her own mind.

" I'm not going to wait here like a lackey in a lobby !" said the doctor, moving towards the door. Cecilia was in a tremour of apprehension.

" Papa, papa ! we can't slip away without bidding the countess good-bye,—without seeing the earl,—it would look so odd, so rude."

"What's odd and rude is their leaving us here,
without paying us common civility! I'll stand it no
longer!" cried the irascible man; and opening the
door, he proceeded along the corridor which led to
the hall, followed by his expostulating daughter.

Unfortunately, their course lay past the library;
and more unfortunately still, the library door happened to be very slightly ajar.

"Can't you manage some way of getting rid of
these miserable Bardons?" were the words, pronounced in an irritated tone, which struck like a
pistol-shot on the ears of the countess's guests.

It was as though that pistol-shot had exploded a
mine of gunpowder! To the earl's amazement the
library door was suddenly flung wide open, and,
quivering with irrepressible rage, the fiery old doctor
stood before him.

"Manage!" exclaimed Bardon, in a voice of
thunder; "there is little *management* required in
dismissing those who, had they known the despicable
pride which inhabits here, would never have stooped,
—*never have stooped*," he repeated, "to degrade
themselves by crossing your threshold! You have
dared to apply to us the epithet of *miserable*," continued Bardon, bringing out the word as with a
convulsive effort, and fixing his fierce eye upon the
disconcerted peer; "I retort back the opprobrious
term! Who is miserable but the miserable slave of
pride,—the worshipper of rank, the gilded puppet

of society, who claims from his ancestors' name the importance which attaches to nothing of his own? This is the first time, sir, that I have visited you, and it shall be the last,—the last time that you shall have the opportunity of insulting, under your own roof, a gentleman whose pretensions to respect are, at least, as well grounded as yours, and who would not exchange his independence of spirit for all the pomp and pageantry which can never give dignity to their possessor, nor avert from him merited contempt!" With the last words on his lips, Bardon turned and departed; his loud, tramping step echoing along the hall, before the earl had time to recover his breath.

Annabella, agitated and excited, appeared about to hurry after her guests, but with an imperious gesture Dashleigh prevented his wife from doing so. Bitterly mortified at what had occurred, irritated, wounded, and offended, the countess burst into a flood of passionate tears.

Pride reigned triumphant that day in the Hall. He had worked out his evil will. He had steeped hearts in bitter gall; he had loosened the bond between husband and wife; he had brought envy, hatred, malice, and all uncharitableness, to rush in at the breach which he had insidiously made.

The countess spent the rest of the day in her own apartment. She would not appear at her husband's table, nor entertain her husband's guest. She had not learned to bear or to forbear; least of all was she prepared to submit her will to that of her imperious lord. Even when the breach between them appeared to be healed, it left its visible scar behind; the wound was ready to break out afresh, for the soft balm of meekness and love had not been poured upon it, and what else can effectually cure the hurt caused by the envenomed shaft of pride?

CHAPTER VIII.

A BROTHER'S EFFORT.

"Solicit not thy thoughts with matters hid,
  Leave them to God above; him serve and fear.
  . . . . Heaven is for thee too high
  To know what passes there. Be lowly wise."
										MILTON.

" The calm philosopher may analyze
    The elements that form a water-drop;
    But will the faint and thirsty pilgrim stop
  To scan its nature, ere the fount he tries?

  Thus, while the haughty soul God's truth receives
    With cold indifference, reasoning, doubting still,—
    The poor in spirit from the sacred rill
  Drinks life, and, ere he comprehends, believes."

THE red glow of sunset had ceased to light up the latticed windows of the vicarage, or bathe its smooth lawn and thick shrubbery in a crimson glow. The rosy tint of the sky had faded into grey, and the evening mist had begun to rise, but still the vica prolonged his walk on the gravel path in front of hi dwelling. Up and down he slowly paced, with hi hands behind him, his eyes bent on the ground, and an expression of thought—painful thought—upon his benevolent face. Ida passed him on her return from a class, but, contrary to his usual habit, h took no notice of his daughter. Mabel tripped through the open window,—a mode of exit which she usually preferred to the door,—and, running lightly up to her father, locked her arm within his, with a playful remark on his solitary mood. The remark did not call up an answering smile; Mr. Aumerle did not appear even to have heard it, so Mabel, concluding from his manner that he must be composing a funeral sermon, quietly left him to his grave meditations.

At length, with a little sigh, as if he had just arrived at the conclusion of some painful line of reflection, the clergyman turned towards the house, and entering at the door, made his way towards his own little study.

As he had expected, the room was not empty. His brother sat reading at the table by the light of a lamp, which threw into strong relief the classic outline of his handsome features. Aumerle saw not —no mortal could see—the dim, dark form beside him, or mark the gigantic shadow cast over the reader by the bat-like wing extended over him by Pride.

Mr. Aumerle sat down near Augustine in silence. He surveyed his brother some moments with a look of anxious tenderness, then gave a little cough, as if to arouse his attention.

Augustine glanced up from the volume of German philosophy which he had been perusing. He had perhaps an idea that something unpleasant was coming, for he did not choose to commence the conversation.

"My dear Augustine," began Lawrence Aumerle, after another uneasy little cough, "I have been for some time wishing to speak to you on a subject of great interest to us both. You must be aware,— you cannot but feel that the light observation which escaped you to-day at dinner, was of a nature to give me considerable pain."

"What I said about the Bible?" replied his brother. "Well, it was a thoughtless observation, I own; but I certainly never intended to pain you. Your good lady came down upon me so sharp, and gave me such an oratorical cudgelling, that even Ida herself must have confessed that the punishment exceeded the offence."

"Augustine, this is no jesting matter," said his brother.

"I own that I was indiscreet and wrong in talking after that fashion in presence of the girls. Are you not satisfied with that frank confession?"

"I am not satisfied; I cannot be satisfied while I remain in doubt as to whether those careless words did not really express the opinion of my brother. Ever since you have been here on this visit, Augustine, it has seemed to me as if a change had passed over you; you are no longer what you once were. There is not the frank interchange of thought between us that there used to be in former years."

"I am no longer a boy," replied Augustine, leaning carelessly back in his chair.

"When you were a boy," continued Mr. Aumerle, "you used often to express to me your desire to enter the ministry."

"Oh, that's all over," replied Augustine quickly; "my views on many points have changed. I have discovered that there are many paths open to speculative thought besides the dry beaten one which you and all the pious world have been content for generations to tread."

"There is nothing," murmured Pride, "so hateful to an exalted spirit as travelling in a crowd."

"Is it well," said Aumerle, "to wander from the narrow path, in which so many have found happiness in life, and peace in death?"

"There are stumbling-blocks in that path," replied Augustine; "difficulties which it would puzzle even a theologian like yourself to remove, and over which the learned and the zealous have wrangled from time immemorial. How can you explain to me this?" and the young man ran over, with rapid eloquence, one after another of the difficult questions which have for ages put human wisdom to fault. "How can you explain all this?" he repeated, at the close of his argument.

These things are beyond the grasp of the human mind," replied the clergyman; "they are not contrary to reason, but above it."

"Reason is the guide allotted to intellectual man," said Augustine; "I go as far as she leads me, and no further."

"Reason is the guide that leads to the temple of revelation. There is an overwhelming mass of evidence, external and internal, to convince any unprejudiced mind that the Bible is the word of God. Prophecies accomplished, types fulfilled, the divine Spirit breathed through the pages, the unearthly perfection of One character there portrayed, with superhuman knowledge of the frailties and requirements of man; the devotion of the early witnesses to its truth, who sealed their testimony with their blood; the standing miracles foretold in the Scriptures, of the Jewish people scattered amongst all nations, and yet separate, and of a Church which, rising in an obscure land from the tomb of its Founder, has spread against the opposition of earth and hell, has swept away the barriers raised against it by temporal power and spiritual idolatry, and the natural opposition of every unregenerate heart, and which still goes on conquering and to conquer;—is not all this sufficient to bring reason to the position of the handmaid of religion, and make her, as I said at the first, the guide to the temple of revelation?"

"Granted," said Augustine, after a pause; "but, when we enter that temple, when we scrutinize the mysteries which it contains—"

"Reason is no longer capable of guiding the soul ; the appointed guardian of these mysteries is faith."

"Who would lead us blindfold!" said Augustine impatiently. "Here it is that I would make my stand, for I maintain that no man— "

Pride.—"Gifted, intellectual man—"

Augustine.—" Is bound to believe what he cannot understand!"

Aumerle.—" Augustine, Augustine, all nature refutes you! What do we understand of the physical wonders that have environed man for thousands of years? We note facts, but in what innumerable instances are we baffled when we attempt to trace back effects to their causes! We hear the power of electricity in the thunder-clap, see it in the flash of lightning, nay, make it the servant of our will to unite distant continents together; but who can say that he understands it? We give it a name, we calculate its force, but reason grasps not its nature. Who can say how the soul is united to the body? Who can say what the faculty of memory may be, where it hoards up its life-accumulated treasures, and produces on the moment from the mass the very idea which it requires? These are not foreign subjects, they are subjects brought daily to the attention of myriads of reasoning beings, and during sixty centuries what has reason made of them? She is content to give up her place to faith; we believe, but we *cannot* understand. And can we expect that aught else should be the case when a weak, helpless worm-like man fixes his thoughts upon the solemn mysteries of the invisible world,—when the finite attempts to comprehend the infinite! Reason, your boasted reason, at once shows the folly of such an expectation. On this earth we are in the infancy of our existence. As little could the young child of a monarch, while scarcely yet able to read, expect to grasp the difficult science of administration, and make himself master of the details of the business of an empire, as man, with his limited faculties, fathom the deep things of God!"

"In this your favourite simile," said Augustine, "you must admit that some children are more advanced than the rest."

"I believe that he is most advanced in spiritual knowledge," replied Aumerle, "who can adopt the language of the gifted warrior-king of Israel." He opened the Bible which lay on the table, and read aloud from the 131st Psalm :—

"*Lord, my heart is not haughty, nor mine eyes lofty : neither do I exercise myself in great matters, or in things too high for me. Surely I have behaved and quieted myself, as a child that is weaned of his mother: my soul is even as a weaned child.*"

"One would almost think," observed Augustine, "that you consider intellect as rather a disqualification than a help in penetrating the mysteries of religion."

F

" These mysteries are beyond the province allotted to human intellect," replied his brother. "The Bible assures us that *the natural man receiveth not the things of God, for they are spiritually discerned.* Our Lord thanked his Father that these things, being hidden *from the wise and prudent* (wise in the world's wisdom, prudent in their own eyes), were yet *revealed unto babes.* Depend upon it, my dear brother," continued the clergyman earnestly, " the true stumbling-block in our path is our pride! Is it not written in the word, *The meek will he guide in judgment, and the meek will he teach his way?*"

"Do you mean to assert," said Augustine, "that none of the meek and devout have ever been troubled with difficulties and doubts?"

"Not so; I believe that many of God's best servants have been much exercised with such spiritual trials. But it has been beautifully written, 'A sign is granted to the doubt of love which is not given to the doubt of indifference.' The meek are not left in darkness,— such are not given up to the adversary. But it is because they oppose him, not in the intellectual armour of subtle reasoning and metaphysical argument, but armed with the sling of prayer, humble and persevering prayer. To such the promise of the Comforter is given, whose office is to guide unto all truth.'"

Augustine.—" You, doubtless, are amongst those spiritually enlightened, though I suspect that you regard me as still in darkness. I should like to know how far, with faith your infallible guide, you have penetrated into such a mystery, for instance, as that of the origin of sin."

Pride.—"Nail him with that difficulty; wrest his one weapon out of his hand, and see how he comes off in the contest when your intellect fairly grapples with his!"

Aumerle.—"I find it more profitable, my brother, to trace the effects of sin in my own heart, than to dive into such a mystery. The existence of sin within us concerns us more nearly than its origin."

Augustine.—"Now own to me frankly, Lawrence, whether there be not something conventional and strained in this perpetual talk—I had almost said *cant*—about sin, which we hear from the best people in the world? I look upon it as the affectation of humility, because without that crowning virtue the most saintly character is not considered to be absolutely perfect."

Aumerle.—" Can you doubt the all-pervading influence of sin? *The heart is deceitful above all things and desperately wicked. All our righteousnesses are as filthy rags. There is none that doeth good, no not one;* this is the scriptural estimate of human nature."

Augustine.—" Lay aside the Scriptures for a moment, and come to actual facts as we see them around us. Look now at such a character as that of

Ida—pure, unworldly, self-denying, devoted; such a description of evil cannot for a moment be applied to her."

Aumerle.—"You see her, God be praised, as she is by grace, and not by nature."

Augustine.—"But she continues to regard herself as a sinner,—for aught that I know as the chief of sinners, she is ever repenting of errors which no one but herself can perceive."

Aumerle.—"With faculties as limited as ours, our not perceiving errors is no proof of their non-exist-ence. What to the naked eye is so pure as a crystal stream, or so glorious as the orb of day? yet the microscope reveals to us impurities in the water, and the telescope—blots in the sun."

Augustine (smiling).—"Leave to me the unassisted vision. I do not wish to think ill of human nature. I believe that a man may walk serenely through life, and find himself in heaven at the end of it, without this incessant judging and condemning either himself or his fellow-creatures."

Pride.—"Yes; one who is like yourself possesses an unblemished character, and a high moral standard, and who seeks to benefit his kind, without professions of superior sanctity."

Aumerle.—"Augustine, I see but too clearly why your mind delights to seek out only the difficulties and doubts in religion! You can sit tranquilly as a judge, because you have never recognised your position as a criminal. You are, with all your brilliant intellect, ignorant of the very alphabet of spiritual knowledge. You do not know your own weakness and sin."

Pride.—"He imagines himself addressing one of the ignorant rustics of his parish. His mind is narrowed by professional bigotry. It requires at least the virtue of patience to listen to such illiberal cant."

Augustine (smiling).—" It seems, Lawrence, that you would have me acknowledge myself not only a child, but a very naughty child."

Aumerle.—"Augustine, this is no subject for trifling. The difference between our ages long made me regard you rather as a beloved son than a brother. In some points our relative positions may be reversed. You have shown yourself to be possessed of talents to which I can lay no claim; I cheerfully cede to you the palm in all that regards intellectual power. But in one thing riper years still give me the advantage. Experience is the natural growth of time; spiritual experience of self-examination and prayer. I am persuaded that every step of the Christian's life opens to him a wider prospect of the evil of his sinful nature. He learns it not only from the Bible, but by painful remembrance of broken resolutions, neglected duties, and secret backslidings, even if the Almighty preserve him from falls visible to others. Spiritual pride, nay, all pride, can be but the offspring of ignorance, ignorance of the requirements of God's

law, and of our failure in fulfilling that law,—ignorance of the infinite holiness of the Creator, and of
the infirmity and guilt of the creature!"

Pride started at the words of Aumerle; and fiercely
shook his sable wing. The earnestness and tenderness of the clergyman's manner might have made
some impression on his brother, but Pride threw
himself between them, and laid an iron grasp on his
slave. Oh, how difficult is it to speak rebuke, without arousing the demon of Pride, and arming his giant
strength against us!

Augustine rose from his seat, and said coldly,
"Lawrence, we have had enough of this, and more
than enough. Thanks for your well-meant sermon,
though it savours more of the musty volumes of old
divinity, than the enlightened systems of an age of
progress. You and I will never look upon these
matters in the same light; let the subject be dropped
henceforth between us!" And so saying, and taking
with him his philosophical book, Augustine Aumerle
quitted the study.

The vicar remained behind, sad, disappointed,
almost disheartened. His words appeared to have
had no effect but that of irritating his brother, and
weakening the bond between them. But Aumerle
had another resource, and he failed not to avail
himself of it. While Augustine in the drawing-
room was amusing himself and delighting his nieces
by a playful critique upon Tennyson's poetry (theology

he had determined carefully to avoid entering upon again at the vicarage), Lawrence was upon his knees in his study, fervently imploring his heavenly Father to open the eyes of one who appeared to be gifted with all knowledge except that which could alone make him *wise unto salvation !*

Perhaps the minister's present failure was to himself a blessing. It was sent to humble and prove him, to make him feel how powerless he was to influence a single soul without the aid of God's Holy Spirit. It made him more earnest in prayer, more fervent in supplication. How many in a better world may find that they have reason to thank God, not only for their successes, but their failures, and see that the blessings which they had invoked upon others, had been returned a hundred-fold into their own bosoms !

CHAPTER IX.

DISAPPOINTMENT.

"Bitterest to the lip of pride,
When hopes presumptuous fade and fall."
                                        KEBLE.

"Save me alike from foolish pride,
    Or impious discontent
For what Thy wisdom hath denied,
    Or what Thy goodness lent!"
                                        POPE.

THE Countess of Dashleigh sat in her boudoir,
surrounded by all the luxuries which art can devise
or wealth procure. But she paid little attention to
anything around her, for her thoughts were absorbed
in her occupation,—to a young authoress a very
delightful occupation,—that of revising the proof-
sheets of her first romance. "Egeria" was now
taking a flight above the columns of a periodical;
she was about to present to the world a volume in
violet and gold! How to give her ideas the richest
setting, how to display her talent to most advantage,
was now the one prevailing thought which occupied
her mind from morning till night. Annabella was
like a mother rejoicing over a first-born child; and
she examined the rough proofs with the interest and
delight which a young parent might feel in surveying

the little elegancies of the wardrobe of her darling babe.

"Egeria" smiled to herself as she imagined the various reviews of her work which would doubtless appear in the papers and periodicals of the day. She fancied what passages would be extracted, what characters praised; what might possibly be censured, what must be admired. In the midst of her enjoyment of this feast of imagination, she was interrupted by the entrance of the earl. Alas! that the presence of a husband should ever be felt unwelcome!

"Anabella, my love, I have just received a letter, which I should be obliged by your answering for me. I am glad to find you with a pen in your hand."

"Presently, Reginald; I will answer it presently," said the countess, a slight frown of impatience passing over her brow; "I am most exceedingly busy at present."

"What are you doing?" inquired the earl, who was not in the secret of his lady's occupation, though aware that she devoted much time to her pen. "May I see?" he added, taking up one of the dirty proof-sheets which had just received Annabella's corrections.

"Are you to be my first critic?" said the countess playfully; "if so, I hope that you will be an indulgent one."

The earl looked for a few minutes a little embarrassed, as if a subject had been suddenly brought

before him on which he had not had time to make
up his mind. He then seated himself on the sofa,
and twisting the paper about in his fingers as he
addressed his wife without looking at her, he began
in his somewhat formal style :—"It seems to me,
Annabella, that authorship is not what is most
exactly suitable for one who holds the position of a
countess."

"Are countesses then supposed to be more stupid
than other people?" asked Annabella.

The earl made no direct reply to a question which
appeared to him rather impertinent. He was
desirous to avoid an argument, and rather to have
recourse to persuasion. "You have so many other
resources," he began, "so many pleasures—"

"Not one of them,—not all of them together to be
compared to this !" exclaimed Annabella with anima-
tion. "I value the smallest bay-leaf from Parnassus
more than the strawberry-leaves on a ducal coronet !"

The Earl of Dashleigh was offended. "I am
aware, madam," he said stiffly, "that you take a
pride in disparaging the advantages of high social
standing. A lofty position has no charms for you."

"I have known the time, Dashleigh," said his
wife, laughing, but with something of bitterness in
her mirth, "when a lofty position had no charms for
you. When you stood upon a certain Swiss mountain, able neither to get upwards nor downwards,
and glad of the assistance of my little hand—"

"That has nothing on earth to do with the question!" cried the earl, colouring and looking angry.

"Oh! I beg your lordship's pardon; I was going to draw an analogy, as the learned say; I was going to make a metaphor of a fact. I looked at snowy peaks, deep abysses, awful chasms, and was transported with a sense of their grandeur, as you are with that of hereditary rank! Mont Blanc seemed to me loftier—more sublime—than the woolsack appears to you! You, on the contrary, grew a little dizzy,—you only considered the fatigue of the climbing, and the danger—"

"This is idle talk!" cried the earl impatiently. "I happened to be taken with a fit of vertigo, and —and of course you have no intention of publishing?" he inquired, making a very abrupt turn in the conversation.

"Of course I have," replied Annabella.

"You do not mean to—to let me infer for a moment that you, the Countess of Dashleigh, have ever dreamed of deriving any pecuniary advantage—" The words appeared almost to choke him, so he left the sentence incomplete.

"You do not suppose that I intend to make a present to the publisher of the effusions of my genius," said the lady. "No, I have the pleasure of working for a good cause. The new gallery of our church is to be propped up by this little pen!"

and with some pride Annabella held upright on the table the small instrument of her literary power.

"Really, madam, you astonish me!" exclaimed the peer, rising in surprise and indignation. "The Countess of Dashleigh to enter the lists with Grub Street penny-a-liners,—the Countess of Dashleigh to receive payment from a publisher, to earn a miserable pittance like any wretched mechanic—"

"To do what Shakspeare, Milton, Johnson, did before her."

"They were not of the peerage," interrupted Dashleigh.

"No, they were something more!" exclaimed Annabella. "They were 'below the good how far; but *far above the great!*' I should be only too proud to follow in their steps!"

"I tell you it is impossible,—utterly impossible," repeated the earl. "My wife to work for hire! I could never show my face again in the House of Lords if I submitted to such a degradation!"

Poor Annabella was like a child whose high-built house of cards has been suddenly dashed to the ground. Her eyes filled fast with tears, but she was too proud to let them overflow.

The earl was not a hard man. He saw that he had given pain, and hastened to smoothe down his young wife's disappointment.

"Since writing gives you such amusement," he said, "I will not altogether discourage it. You may print that work for private circulation—I have no great objection to that—and as for the gallery of the church, I will support that by a handsome donation."

Dashleigh thought that this concession must entirely satisfy Annabella, but in this he showed little knowledge of the peculiar ambition of his wife. What! was she never to see a review of her work in a leading paper,—was she to limit its circulation, —were a few friends and acquaintance alone to enjoy what she had expected would excite a sensation throughout the literary world! This would be clipping the wings of her Pegasus indeed, and making him the mere carriage-horse of a peer!

"I would rather burn my volume at once," she said pettishly, "than have it merely printed for private circulation. I should be ashamed to send it round like a begging-box to my acquaintance, with an understood petition of 'compliments thankfully received!'"

"You could not endure to see your book hawked about, sold on miserable stalls, thumbed in circulating libraries!"

The idea was shocking to the earl, but very delightful to Annabella. "I could endure it very well," she said coldly; "I see no harm in the thing."

But I see it, madam," exclaimed Dashleigh, "and what's more, I will not suffer it to be done! Your dignity is connected with my own; it may be nothing to you, but it is something to me. If my wishes have no effect, you will at least listen to my commands."

"Tyrant!" whispered the demon Pride; and the heart of Annabella echoed the treasonous word 'tyrant!'"

The earl was satisfied with having taken a step so decided. He had no wish to prolong a discussion with his wife, in which, as he knew by experience, she generally had the advantage. Having uttered his mandate he quitted the room, leaving Annabella in a state of angry excitement.

"Private circulation! I may print for private circulation! most condescending concession from my lord!" she muttered to herself, as she sat gloomily surveying the proofs which had lately afforded her such keen delight. Then a thought seemed at once to strike the countess, her over-cast countenance lighted up with a gleam as if of triumph. "Yes; I will write something for private circulation," she cried, "something which my lord will find so very amusing, so highly diverting, that he will be glad to compound for its suppression by letting me do what I like with my book. Mine shall be a little romance in real life, an incident in the life of a peer of the realm!" and, dashing the drops from her eyes, Annabella at once sat down to her desk.

She wrote in a fit of resentment, and what she penned naturally took the colour of her feelings. The countess wrote a ludicrous account of a little ad-

venture which had occurred to the Earl of ———, the
dash serving as a transparent veil which every one
could see through. She recounted how the earl, ac-
companied by his wife, who was fired with the ambition of emulating the feats which Albert Smith has
rendered famous, ascended part of the way up a
Swiss mountain. She described how, long ere the
snowy region was reached, the nobleman had been
seized with giddiness and nervous fear; how he had
stood on a steep slope, with a precipice on either
hand, clutching tremblingly at the rock-plants which
gave way in his grasp, calling out in alarm for aid,
and thankful at last to catch hold of the end of a
boa which his more active and fearless partner extended from the summit of a cliff. It was a relief
to Annabella to give vent to her anger and malice
in this little, humorous sketch. She wrote without
any deliberate intention of ever showing it to a
human eye; her paper took to her the place of a
female confidante, that too often mischievous companion to a woman who is not happily married.

Having finished her little piece the countess descended to the drawing-room, to pass a sullen, uncomfortable evening in the society of her aristocratic
husband.

CHAPTER X.

ON THE WATCH.

"Struggling in the world's dark strife,
  Man requires, ere parting thence,
Pardon for the holiest life,
  For the purest—penitence.

Helpless all—a Power above
  Saving strength alone can give,
Sinners all,—a God of love
  Only bids the guilty live!
From polluted works we flee,
  Lord, to hide ourselves in Thee!"

IT was a sunny afternoon in April. In a rustic arbour at the end of the garden, garlanded with honey-
suckle and clematis, through the interstices of whose
bright, young leaves came the smiling sunshine, and
the soft breath of Spring, sat Ida and Mabel Aumerle.
This arbour was a favourite retreat of the girls;
thither they carried their books and their work;
and could the clustering shrubs around it have had
a voice, much could they have told of sweet converse
held together by the sisters, and that free interchange
of thought which is one of the dearest privileges of
friendship.

"Ida, dearest," said Mabel, "shall I tell you what
Uncle Augustine said of you to-day when you left

the room after prayers? He said, 'Ida is a noble girl, and has no fault except that of being too good.' Papa smiled and shook his head gently; Mrs. Aumerle gave her odious, little shrug!"

"Uncle Augustine does not know my heart," said Ida.

"But I know it if any one does, and I am sure that uncle himself cannot think more highly of you than I do."

"You are partial," replied her sister with a smile.

"I only wish that I were like you! I know I'm a proud, wayward girl, and shall never reach heaven unless I am better. I often make good resolutions, but somehow"—Mabel looked down sadly as she spoke,—"somehow they break away like thread in the flame! I wonder if I shall ever be really holy."

Ida laid down the muslin which she was working, and drawing closer to her young sister, said in a gentle tone, "You speak, dearest, of being holy and reaching heaven; of making good resolutions and not being able to keep them,—as if the impression were on your mind that you have to form, as it were, a ladder of good works, by which to reach a certain difficult height, beyond which lie the regions of glory."

'That's just it," said Mabel sadly, "and I am discouraged because I always find that my ladder is too short; that climb as I may, I never can reach the height that you do."

G

"I threw away my ladder long ago," said Ida clasping her hands ; "I found that every round in it was broken!"

"O Ida, what do you mean? I am certain that you have never ceased to do good works daily."

"I would no more use them," exclaimed Ida, "as *a means of reaching heaven*, than I would hope, by aid of yonder fragile clematis, to climb to the bright sun or stars! No," she continued, her lip trembling with emotion as she spoke, "I would put those works which you call good, to the only use for which they are fit if the fire of love kindle the broken, imperfect fragments, I may humbly offer upon them a sacrifice of thanksgiving to Him through whom alone I have hope of reaching the heavenly heights."

"But, Ida, I can hardly yet see how *every round* on the ladder of good works is broken. I am sure that some—at least of *yours*, must be very pleasing to God."

"Let us examine them closely," replied Ida, "let us fix upon what you consider the very best of our works, and let us see if it could, even for a moment, in itself support the weight of a soul."

Mabel considered for a little, and then said, "Perhaps the best of our works is prayer."

"We shall not need much examination, I fear, to find that our prayers are cold, wandering, insincere."

"Cold sometimes, yes,—but —"

"And sadly wandering," added Ida; "at least I

am sure that I feel mine to be so. O Mabel! I have often reflected that if an angel could write down all the thoughts that flow through our minds while we kneel in the attitude of prayer,—the foolish fancies, the idle dreams, the vain selfish imaginations which mix with our earnest supplications, we should be so shocked and disgusted at such a mockery of devotion, that with penitence and shame we should implore that our prayers themselves should be forgiven!"

"Yes; they are cold and wandering,—but I am sure that mine are not insincere."

"I am afraid that we sometimes ask for blessings which we have no earnest desire to obtain. Do we not sometimes pray to be delivered from pride and uncharitableness, when at the time we are fostering these enemies as welcome guests in our hearts? Have we fully entered into the spirit of that prayer which we have so often uttered:—

> 'The dearest idol I have known,
> Whate'er that idol be,
> Help me to tear it from thy throne,
> And worship only Thee?'

If we were quite certain that such prayers would be granted *directly*, would we not sometimes be afraid to breathe them, and is there then no insincerity in having them so frequently on our lips?"

"O Ida!" exclaimed Mabel, with a sigh; "you look a great deal too closely into the heart! If our very prayers be full of sin, what must our worldly actions be? The most disagreeable duty in the

world is this searching for hidden evil, this dreadful
self-examination! I am sure that a great many
good people never practise it, and are much happier
for their ignorance of themselves."

"What should we say, dear one, of a man of business who refused to look into his books, lest he
should find the balance against him? of the owner
of a dwelling who should be content to keep one
room swept and cleansed, leaving all the rest, with
locked doors and closed shutters, to darkness and pol-
lution? what should we think of the governor of a
castle, who should pace proudly along the battlements, careless whether a lurking foe had not penetrated to the heart of the fortress?"

"I should certainly think the two first fools, and
the third a traitor to his trust," replied Mabel. "But,
Ida, this self-examination only makes us miserable!
If I find every round in my ladder broken, and have
my fierce enemy behind me, and before me the
heights which I shall never be able to reach,—what
can I do but sit down and despair?"

"You forget, you forget," cried Ida, with anima-
tion, "the bright golden cord which is let down to
you from above. We cannot climb to heaven by our
good works; but faith, living, loving faith, can grasp
the means of salvation held out by a merciful
Saviour. The more helpless we feel ourselves, the
more eagerly we cling to our only sure hope. Mabel, this is the glory of the Gospel. It humbles the

sinner, but exalts the Saviour ; it shows us that we can do nothing in ourselves, yet can do all things through Him who loved and gave himself for us !"

Mabel made no reply in words, but she drooped her head till it found its resting-place on a sister's bosom. An arm was gently drawn around her, and Ida imprinted a silent kiss on her brow. The demon Pride stood gloomily aloof ; he felt himself baffled for a time, and dared not intrude his presence on the sisters during the remainder of that peaceful day !

CHAPTER XI.

THE QUARREL.

"A something light as air,—a look,
  A word unkind, or wrongly taken,
Oh! love that tempests never shook
  A breath, a touch like this hath shaken!
And ruder words will soon rush in
To spread the breach that words begin,
And eyes forget the gentle ray
They wore in courtship's smiling day,
And voices lose the tone that shed
A tenderness o'er all they said;—
Till fast declining, one by one
The sweetnesses of love are gone,
And hearts, so lately mingled, seem
Like broken clouds, or like the stream
That smiling leaves the mountain's brow,
  As though its waters ne'er could sever,
Yet, ere it reach the plain below,
  Breaks into floods, that part for ever!"

MOORE.

THE Earl and Countess of Dashleigh now found less
enjoyment in the mutual converse which had once
made their days flow so pleasantly and swiftly, and
which had been especially appreciated by Dashleigh,
whose reserve or pride made him avoid much general
society.   When Annabella's wit sparkled before him,
he had needed no other amusement, and in the first
part of her wedded life, she had required no other
auditor than him who listened with so partial an ear.
But each now felt that a change had come, as water

penetrating the crevices of a rock, and then freezing, sometimes by its sudden expansion bursts asunder the solid stone, and severs it as effectually by silent power as a gunpowder blast could have done, so secret pride in both hearts was gradually, fatally dividing those bound to each other by the closest of earthly ties! There was yet, however, no open quarrel; the world was not called in as a spectator of domestic disunion. There was no appearance of want of harmony as, on the occasion which I am about to relate, the husband and the wife sat together in the countess's luxurious boudoir, Annabella on a damask sofa, engaged in German work, the earl at a writing-table, looking over a copy of the *Times*.

There had been a long silence between them. It was broken by a question from Dashleigh.

"Did you know, Annabella, that Augustine Aumerle was soon going to leave the vicarage and return to Aspendale?"

"I know little of what goes on at the vicarage," replied Annabella, after pausing to count stitches in her pattern; "I think that Ida must have cut me, she so seldom comes to the hall."

"There are to be great doings at Aspendale," resumed Dashleigh; "I saw Augustine this morning during my ride, and he told me of his novel arrangements. He expects soon a visit from Verdon, the well-known aeronaut; I wonder that he keeps up acquaintance with one who may be regarded as a public exhibitor; but that is his business, not mine; it seems that they were school-fellows together, and it is not easy to break off old friendships."

"If there be such a thing as a *lofty* profession it is Mr. Verdon's, without doubt," said Annabella; "the aspirations of an aeronaut must mount higher than even those of a peer!"

"It appears," continued Dashleigh, without seeming to take notice of the observation, "that Mr. Verdon is to give his new grand balloon a trial trip from Augustine's grounds."

"Oh, how I should like to be there!" cried the countess.

"Augustine has invited us both,"—Annabella clapped her hands like a child,—" but the difficulty is that he will not be able himself to do the honours of his house, as he is to accompany Verdon in his upward flight."

"Is he?" exclaimed the young countess; "that will be charming! Such a genius will mount up so high, that the silken ball will have no need of hydrogen gas! He will but inflate it with poetical ideas, and it will never stop short of the stars!"

The earl smiled at the idea. "I should be well pleased to see the ascent," he observed; "but yet I am doubtful about accepting the invitation. It would, you see, be awkward for those in our position of life to be guests at the table of a man who was at the moment up in the clouds."

Annabella burst into a girlish laugh. " You are afraid that he might look down even upon us," she cried.

" I doubt whether etiquette would allow—"

" Throw etiquette to the dogs !" exclaimed Annabella, heedless of her husband's look of disgust at such an audacious parody on Shakspeare. " I must, will go to Aspendale ! It will be such fun ! I have half a mind to ascend in the balloon myself !"

It would be very unsuitable for a lady," began the earl,—

" Unless her lord would accompany her," said Annabella, archly ; " we might obtain as fine a view as from Mont Blanc, without all the trouble of climbing."

The earl always winced under any allusion to his mountain adventure.

" But then," continued Annabella maliciously, " it would never do to get giddy,—suspended between earth and sky,—there would be no hope of the friendly intervention of a lady's boa !"

" I should not have the slightest objection, not the slightest," repeated the irritated earl, " to go in a balloon to-morrow ; indeed, I think it very probable that I shall make one of Augustine's party."

Annabella was diverted to see that she had succeeded in putting her haughty lord on his mettle.

It seems an instinct with some natures to delight in
showing a power to tease, and it had become stronger
with the countess since her disappointment regarding her romance.   She was like a child playing with
fire-arms, ignorant of their dangerous nature.   Annabella knew the weakness of her husband's nerves, but
not the full strength of his pride.

"I was reading yesterday a curious account of a
balloon ascent," continued the earl, in a quieter tone;
"and, by-the-bye, I have not quite finished it.   It
is in the —— Magazine; have you seen the last
number, Annabella ?"

"I glanced over it," replied the lady, carelessly;
"I suppose that it is lying on one of the tables."

The earl rose and looked around for the magazine.   His wife was too busy in arranging the
shades for a withered rose-leaf to give him the least
assistance.   She was too busy to notice that he at
length extended his search for the missing periodical
to the drawer of her writing-table.   Into that drawer,
with habitual carelessness, the countess had thrust a
little manuscript, to which, after hastily writing it,
she had scarcely given a thought.

"What's this ?" exclaimed Dashleigh half aloud
as his gaze unwittingly fell upon the title—"The
Precipice and the Peer."   The first glance had been
purely accidental, for the earl was above petty curiosity, and would never have touched either paper or
drawer had he supposed them to contain anything

secret. But now an ungovernable impulse made him open the leaves, and hastily run his eye over the contents. Annabella had just succeeded in finding a missing shade of russet, when she was startled by a sudden sound resembling a stamp; and looking up, she saw the earl with his very temples crimsoned by rage, and her unfortunate burlesque in his hand.

"Lord Dashleigh!" exclaimed the countess, "that was never intended—"

"Never intended for my eye!" thundered the earl, who was in a violent passion; and tearing the manuscript into a hundred pieces, he trampled it under his foot!

"That is the action of a pettish child!" exclaimed Annabella, almost as much irritated as her husband, her eyes flashing indignant fire.

"Leave the room, insolent girl!" cried the earl; and turning round as he spoke, he perceived to his surprise and inexpressible annoyance that he had two unexpected auditors—his servant having a moment before opened the door, to announce the Duke of Montleroy, who was following close behind!

Dashleigh was so much confused—overwhelmed at being discovered by such a person in such a position—that of a husband quarrelling with his own wife, and giving way to a burst of passion degrading to any man, but most of all to one of his exalted station—that he remained for some minutes transfixed, totally unable to speak. Annabella, on the contrary, lost none of her self-possession. She swept past the bewildered duke, with a passing reverence which might have beseemed an empress, and proceeded at once to her own chamber, without uttering a word. As soon as she had reached it, she violently rang her bell.

The maid who obeyed the summons found her mistress sitting at her toilette table, calm, tearless, but pale with suppressed emotion. She was selecting various articles of jewellery from a large mahogany box.

"Bates, bid the coachman put the horses to directly, and do you prepare to accompany me in the carriage," was the countess's brief command.

The lady had, not an honr before, returned from a lengthened drive, and the order surprised the maid. She ventured to say something about the late hour and the appearance of coming rain.

"Let it rain torrents—what matters it?" cried Annabella. "Bear my message to Mullins, and return without delay to pack up the things which I shall require. I shall sleep at the vicarage to-night."

The lady's-maid hurried away to the servant's hall, which she found in a state of considerable excitement, for the news had already spread like wildfire through the house that my lord had quarrelled with my lady, torn up her writings, ordered her out of the room—nay, as it was rumoured, had actually struck her on the face.

"Take my word for it," cried the butler, with the air of one who can see much further through a mill-stone than others,—"take my word for it this has something to do with the odd couple as came here the other day,—the fine lady, and the fierce old man with black brows and long white hair."

"Yes," replied another servant, with a nod, "I've noticed that nothing has gone right up stairs since them two drove off in the donkey-chaise, and my lady shut herself up in her room, as if she'd had a down-right set-down from my lord."

"Oh, for the matter of that," laughed Bates, "she'd give as good as she gets, any day. The earl has ordered her out of the room; but she's going a little further than may be he wished or expected. She has a spirit of her own, has my lady!"

In the meantime, Annabella was pacing up and down her apartment with a heart full almost to bursting. "I will not stay here, no, not an hour!" she exclaimed; "he shall find that he has no weak girl to deal with—no slave to submit to his pride and caprice! I have borne much, but this I will not bear. I will not endure to be trampled upon by a tyrant, even though that tyrant be a husband. I will go to the vicarage at once. Mr. Aumerle will not forget that my mother was the sister of the wife whom he loved. He will not deny the shelter of his roof to an orphan, so cruelly driven from her own. I will impose no burden upon my friends. I ask, I need nothing from any one but the sympathy which my griefs, and the justice which my wrongs demand."

Thus, asking counsel only of her own angry passions, casting aside all higher considerations, and seeking but the gratification of her bitter pride and resentment, the young Countess of Dashleigh prepared to take a step which scarcely any circumstances could justify. Intoxicated as she was with anger, the voice of reason and of conscience were alike unheard or unheeded. Indignant at the errors of her husband, Annabella was blinded to her own ; and when she found her domestic happiness wrecked, her youthful hopes scattered like leaves in a storm, she recognised not the cause of the evil—she traced not in the desolation around her the work of the demon Pride.

CHAPTER XII.

THE UNEXPECTED GUEST.

"Chill falls the rain,
Night-winds are blowing;
Dreary and dark is
The way thou'rt going!"

MOORE.

ON that evening, a small but cheerful party were
assembled in the sitting-room of the vicarage. Dr. Bardon and his daughter Cecilia, oft-invited guests, had
joined the circle of the Aumerles. A week never passed
without some little act of kindness being shown by
the clergyman or his family to the disinherited man.
Bardon heartily esteemed, and even felt a warm regard for the vicar. But let it not be supposed that
he was overburdened with a sense of gratitude for
unwearying kindness and attention. No, he was far
too proud for that. The doctor was ever keeping a
balance in his mind between benefits received and
benefits conferred; and by means of that curious
mental instrument, of which Mabel had penetrated
the secret, he managed always, in his own opinion,
to keep the balance weighed down in his favour. If
the Aumerles showed him hospitality, it was, he
easily persuaded himself, because they were really

glad to have a little society. Bardon did them an
actual favour by so often eating their dinners!
Volunteered advice upon diet and medical subjects,
though given to those whose health was perfect, the
doctor also regarded as obligations of no trivial nature ; and he often calculated how much the Aumerles
owed to him in the shape of fees !

On this evening the mind of Bardon was particularly easy, for he had brought to the vicar the gift
of a crystallized pebble, which he had discovered in
some ancient drawer, and which, he was perfectly
assured, must be a curious geological specimen. The
Aumerles had sufficient of that. politeness which is
" good-nature refined," to humour the fancy of their
guest ; and there was a discussion for nearly twenty
minutes upon the beauties, peculiarities, and supposed
origin of the wonderful stone.

A heavy rain is pattering without, and flashes of
bright lightning are occasionally reflected on the
wall ; but safe in the comfortable dwelling, the party
give little heed to the weather.   In one corner sits
Dr. Bardon, engaged in a game of chess with Mrs.
Aumerle.   He considers that he is giving her a lesson;
she, having no particular desire to learn the game,
and finding no great amusement in an inevitable
check-mate, is good-humouredly submitting to be
beaten for the gratification of her guest.   Cecilia,
rather over-dressed, as usual, as if, as Mabel once
observed, she were always expecting a grand party,

after much persuasion, which she regards as the in-
dispensable prelude to her performance, has passed
her pink ribbon over her neck, and is giving her
friends a song, to the accompaniment of the guitar.
It is with her music as with things more important,
Cecilia, in her efforts to rise above mediocrity, only
manages to sink below it. She is not contented with
the soft middle tones, in which her voice shows considerable sweetness; Cecilia must sing very high;
and the painful result is, that the strained organ cannot reach the prescribed point, falls flat, and discord
annoys the ear. Miss Bardon is not satisfied with
simple ballads, which she could sing with feeling and
taste; she must show off her very indifferent execu-
tion in difficult bravura airs. As her dress must be
that of a peeress, so her music must be that of a pro-
fessor. Cecilia aims not at giving pleasure, but at
exciting admiration, and succeeds in accomplishing
neither object. Poor Ida, a distressed listener to the
flourishes in "Bel raggio lusinghier," is meditating
how she can contrive to unite politeness with truth-
fulness; and in thanking Miss Bardon for her song,
neither violate sincerity nor hurt the feelings of her
sensitive friend. Mabel, who has kept up a low,
whispered conversation with her uncle at the very
farthest end of the room, is impatiently waiting till
Cecilia's cadenzas and appoggiaturas shall cease, to
speak to her father on a subject of which her mind
is quite full.

H

The last twang at length is given; Ida says, what she can say; if it be a little less than the singer would have liked, it is a little more than the speaker's conscience could warrant. Mr. Aumerle's simple thanks have been uttered, and Mabel, released from the necessity of being comparatively quiet, runs up to her father, and says, playfully leaning on his arm; "O papa! I have such a favour, such a great favour to ask of you!"

"If it be anything reasonable."

"I don't know if you'll think it reasonable or not, but Uncle Augustine sees no objections. He says that he will, if you only consent, take me up with him in the balloon!"

"My child!" exclaimed the vicar.

"Bless the girl!" cried Mrs. Aumerle from her chess-board. Cecilia lifted her hands in surprise, while Dr. Bardon laughed aloud.

"O papa! what's the harm? It is not as if a party of strangers were going on the airy excursion,—people who did not know how to manage. Mr. Verdon is so experienced, he has been up fourteen or fifteen times, and no accident ever has happened. Uncle Augustine goes himself!"

"But because Uncle Augustine chooses to risk his own neck sky-larking amongst the clouds, I see no reason why he should carry my little girl with him on a dangerous excursion."

"Shakspeare tells us," said Augustine, coming towards the centre of the room, that

'Tis dangerous to take a cold, to sleep, to drink,'

but the poet adds

'Out of the nettle, danger, we pluck the flower, safety.'

When steam-vessels were first introduced it was thought an act of daring to go in one,—when railroads were yet a novelty it was foolhardiness to venture in a train."

"Perhaps," joined in the eager Mabel, "balloons will some day become as common as carriages !"

"In that case," observed the doctor, "perhaps Miss Mabel will not care to enter one."

Mabel coloured and laughed. "I daresay," she replied, "that there is something in the excitement and danger,—*supposed* danger I mean,—that makes the thought of such a trip so delighful. I should like, I own, to do something which no lady in the county ever has done before."

"That's pride," said her step-mother abruptly.

Such a gush of fierce angry emotion rose in the heart of the young girl at the word, opprobrious and yet so true, that Augustine, perceiving her feelings in her face, and fearing that she might give them vent, thought it as well to effect an immediate diversion. "I hope," said he, turning towards the doctor, "that you and Miss Bardon will honour Aspendale by your presence on the day of the ascent of the *Eaglet.*"

The doctor bowed, for his *sensitiveness* was gratified by the respectful terms in which the invitation
was couched.

"We shall not be a large, but a select party," continued Augustine Aumerle. "I met Reginald Dashleigh to-day, and I think that he and his lady will
come to witness the ascent."

"Do you mean to say that you expect the earl as
one of your guests?" exclaimed Bardon.

"If nothing prevent, I think that you will meet
him at my house."

"Something will prevent!" cried the old lion,
shaking his white mane with haughty disdain. "I
am willing to meet at your table any one else whom
you may choose to invite;—I would sit down with
farmer—ploughboy—pauper, but not—not with
Reginald Earl of Dashleigh!"

An uncomfortable silence instantly fell like cold
water over the circle; the vicar, a peacemaker by
nature as well as profession, was particularly annoyed
by this unexpected declaration of enmity against his
niece's husband, made by one of his own oldest friends.
He was in act to speak, when Mabel suddenly exclaimed, "There is the sound of a carriage!"

"You must be mistaken," said Mrs. Aumerle, "no
one would come at this hour, and especially on so
stormy an evening."

"But it is a carriage," said Mabel, going to the
window, "I see the red liveries of the Dashleighs."

The sentence unconsciously escaped her lip, and she bit it with vexation at having thoughtlessly uttered the name ; for the doctor started up from his seat so hastily, that he upset the chess-table before him.

This created a little noise and confusion, in the midst of which Annabella suddenly entered the room unannounced, looking so haggard and ill, that her uncle involuntary exclaimed, " My dear Anna ! has anything happened ?"

" Might I speak with you for a moment alone," said the countess assuming with effort a forced calmness. The vicar, without reply, took her by the trembling hand, and led her to his own little study.

" Dear me ! how ill the countess looks !" exclaimed Cecilia.

" Something serious has occurred, depend upon it," said Mrs. Aumerle ; and a variety of conjectures arose as to the cause of the lady's strange visit, though most of the party present had the prudence to keep these conjectures to themselves.

The vicar returned after rather a long absence, and his entrance caused a dead silence in the room, while every eye rested on him with a look of inquiry. He appeared very grave, and drawing his wife aside, said in a low tone of voice, " My dear, do you think that Ida could arrange to share Mabel's apartment to-night, and give up her own to Annabella ?"

" Is the countess so unwell that she cannot return

to her own home ?   The weather seems to be clearing," said the vicar's wife in a voice much more
audible than that of her husband had been.

" She does not wish to return," replied Mr. Aumerle
sadly ; " we must all do our best to make her comfortable here, at least for the present."

In a few minutes Ida had glided out of the room,
and was in the study at the side of her cousin, listening with wonder and pain to the passionate outpour-
ings of a wounded spirit.   Cecilia who delighted in
anything mysterious, was endeavouring to draw from
Mabel her opinion as to the cause of the countess's
distress, and Mrs. Aumerle was bustling about to
" make things smooth," as she said, in the household
department, of which the arrangements had been so
suddenly disturbed by the unexpected arrival.

"Something wrong with Dashleigh, I fear," observed Augustine half aloud.

"Something wrong—everything wrong, I should
say !" exclaimed the doctor who overheard him.
" The case is clear enough to any one who has had
a glimpse behind the scenes as I have had.   The
poor little thing is wretched at home, she has sold
her happiness for a title, she has thrown herself away
on the most proud, selfish, domineering—"

" Dashleigh is my friend," interrupted Augustine
sternly.

"I'd rather have him for my enemy than my friend!"
muttered Bardon between his clenched teeth.

CHAPTER XIII.

THE FRIEND'S MISSION.

"Oh, let the ungentle spirit learn from hence,
A small unkindness is a great offence!"
HANNAH MORE.

"DON'T talk to me," cried Mrs. Aumerle, in the tone of decision which to her was habitual; "I say that a young wife does wrong, exceedingly wrong, in leaving the home of her natural protector, and throwing herself back upon her own family, just because she and her husband have chanced to have some unpleasant words together."

The time was the afternoon of the day following that of Annabella's unexpected arrival; the scene was the sitting-room at the vicarage; the auditor, Mabel Aumerle.

"Unpleasant words!" repeated Mabel angrily; "why the earl tore her writing to pieces, and ordered her out of the room, before her own servant—only think of that, before her own liveried servant! No woman of spirit could submit to that!"

"Woman of spirit—nonsense!" cried the step-mother, "a woman's spirit ought to be one of submission."

"I would have done what she did!" said Mabel.

"I daresay that you would," answered Mrs. Aumerle, with a touch of sarcasm in her manner; but I happen to know a good deal more of life than you do, and mind my word, Mabel, when a woman marries she takes her husband for better, for worse; she has made her choice and she must abide by it; she only lowers herself by appealing to the world to arbitrate between her and the man whom she has vowed to obey."

"How has Annabella appealed to the world?" asked Mabel, with but little of respect in her tone.

"By making herself the talk of the world. There's not a house in Pelton, no, nor much farther round, in which the flight of the countess and its cause is not the subject of conversation. The gossips are feasting on the news, and doubtless by to-morrow morning we shall have the whole affair, with every kind of exaggeration, appearing in the county paper. I've really no patience with the girl! And to mix us up with her folly! I feel as if I were aiding and abetting a wife's rebellion against her husband."

"Unfeeling creature!" thought Mabel, whose partiality for her cousin, and high-flown spirit of romance, made her espouse the countess's cause with the chivalric devotion of a knight errant towards some fair and persecuted damsel.

"I am sure I hope that she does not intend to

prolong her stay here," continued Mrs. Aumerle.
"To say nothing, of the inconvenience of accommodat-
ing herself and her fine maid, I think it an evil to
have in the house one who sets such an example of
wilfulness and pride."

"Papa could never but welcome to his home the
orphan niece of my own beloved mother," exclaimed
Mabel, with flashing eyes, feeling as though she were
doing a lofty and generous action in defending the
cause of the oppressed.

"A child of fifteen is no judge of these matters,
and would show her good sense best by her silence,"
was the cold observation of Mrs. Aumerle.

Mabel's proud spirit was thoroughly roused by
this remark. Her present mood seemed strangely
inconsistent with the softened humility which she
had shown, when in the arbour a few days previously,
she had leant her head on her sister's bosom, feeling herself indeed to be a poor, helpless sinner!
But is not this a species of inconsistency which, by
experience, we know to be but too common in the
heart? We prostrate ourselves before God, but
stand erect before our fellow-creatures : we own our
infirmities in the quiet hour when religion speaks to
the soul, but start back with angry indignation,
if those weaknesses be touched upon by another.
Pride stands back when we, in solitude, or with one
chosen friend, review our past conduct and mourn
over our faults, but springs forward if a rebuke,

however just, be not sweetened by flattery, or tempered by caution.

Mabel disliked her stepmother, and did not care to hide that dislike from its object. The feeling partly arose from a want of tenderness and tact on the part of Mrs. Aumerle. That lady, with much common sense, high principle, and warmth of heart, was quite devoid of that nice apprehension of tender points, that delicacy in touching upon painful subjects, which is morally, what *feelers* are physically to some of the insect creation. Mrs. Aumerle had no *feelers*, and she rather prided herself on the want. She classed nerves, sensibility, timidity, romance, under the one comprehensive title of "humbug;" things which, like cobwebs, she would have thought too insignificant to be noticed, had they not been, to the mental eye, too unsightly to be spared. Mrs. Aumerle's sympathies were quick and active in cases of what she regarded as real distress. She was an eminently practical woman, and did much good in her husband's parish; but she had no pity for nervous complaints, no patience for fanciful troubles. It may be imagined how little of congeniality there could be between such a character and that of the refined sensitive Ida, the romantic impulsive Mabel.

But without congeniality there should have been, on the part of the stepdaughters, a just appreciation of merit, meek submission to authority, and due respect of manner. If Mabel, on all these points, was by far the most open offender, Ida, on her part, was assuredly not free from her share of blame. Her youngest sister looked up to her both as a guide and example. Mabel's highest ambition was to copy the character of Ida, and like most young artists, she unintentionally exaggerated all the defects of what she copied. Mabel seemed to have an intuitive perception of the fact that Ida held her stepmother in low estimation, regarded her advice as valueless, took her reproofs almost as wrongs. Ida, unwittingly, was nurturing in her sister a spirit of proud independence, much more congenial, alas! to the human heart, than the faith, humility, and love which the young Christian earnestly sought to implant in her young companion. Ida was to a certain degree counteracting the effects of her own counsels, defeating the aim of her own prayers.

Mabel, on the present occasion, was so much irritated by her stepmother's recommendation of silence, that she was about to utter an insolent reply, when the conversation was fortunately interrupted by the entrance of her father, whose presence ever acted as a check on any ebullition of temper.

"Well, Lawrence," said Mrs. Aumerle, coming forward to meet her husband, "I hope that this unpleasant affair is to come to a speedy end."

"God grant it!" replied the clergyman. "Have you spoken to Annabella?"

"I was beginning to tell her a little of my mind,

when she implored me to leave the room. She has rather too much of the countess about her, to care to listen to simple truth. She was in a highly excited state; I should not wonder if she were in a fever to-morrow."

"Do you think that we should send for Dr. Bardon?"

"He'll come, sure enough, without our sending. We shall have no peace as long as the countess remains here. All the idle, curious people in the county will find some excuse for visiting the vicarage. The Greys, Whitemans, and Barclays have been here to-day already. I have given Mary orders to let in nobody but the Doctor."

"Is Ida with her cousin?" asked Aumerle.

"She has hardly been out of her room from the first."

"That is well," said the vicar; "my child will do her best to calm and to soften."

"I think that it is the earl who must require to be calmed and softened," observed Mrs. Aumerle; "he has been very shamefully treated."

"Augustine has, as you are aware, undertaken a mission to him. I would have gone myself, but my brother's greater intimacy with Dashleigh, and superior powers of persuasion, would, I felt, make him a more effectual advocate for this poor misguided young creature. I thought that he would have been back ere now. I await his return with great anxiety."

" Here comes my uncle !" exclaimed Mabel.

Aumerle met his brother at the door. "Any good tidings?" he exclaimed. Augustine shook his head doubtingly as they entered the sitting-room together.

" The earl is extremely indignant," he said, removing the hat from his heated brow; "I have been arguing with him for more than an hour, and I have my doubts as to whether we have come to a satisfactory conclusion at last."

" Oh, on what does he decide?" cried Mabel.

" He consents at length to pardon the countess's act of foolish petulance, on condition that she ask his forgiveness, and return this very day to her home."

" Reasonable terms !" said Mrs. Aumerle.

" Yes," assented the vicar, but the little furrow of anxious thought still remained on his brow. "Augustine," he said to his brother, "will you go and communicate your message to Annabella?"

" Nay, nay, I have done my part. If I have more influence with my old college-companion, you have more power with your niece. I suspect that your task will be at least as difficult as mine, notwithstanding your gentle auxiliaries. I have so little expectation of your success, that I have ordered a conveyance to take me to Aspendale an hour hence, that I may leave your dwelling more free to accommodate its new guest."

" I hope," said Mrs. Aumerle, " that the cou-

veyance will rather be required to take Annabella
back to the home which she should never have
quitted."

"I hope so too," observed Augustine with a smile;
"but I own that I have my doubts and my fears on
the matter."

The vicar at once proceeded to the room in which
Ida was endeavouring, though with little effect, to
soothe the irritated spirit of her cousin. Annabella
rose on the clergyman's entrance, and Ida, from
a feeling of delicacy, silently left the apartment.

Aumerle gently communicated to his impatient
auditor the message which he bore.

"His pardon!" exclaimed Annabella, "striking
her little hand with vehemence on a table which was
beside her; "his pardon, forsooth! and for what?
Nay, then, I see the truth of the words—

> 'Forgiveness to the injured doth belong,
> He never pardons who hath done the wrong,'"

and she laughed in the bitterness of her soul.

"My dear niece," said the vicar tenderly but
gravely, "even by your own account you had given
just cause of displeasure to your husband, before he
spoke the hasty word which you find it so difficult to
forgive. Prejudice may blind you—"

"Uncle, let me have no more of this; I can't bear
it!" exclaimed Annabella, rising in nervous excitement. "If I am in your way—in Mrs. Aumerle's
way, I will leave the house at once, go to London

—an hotel—anywhere—but I will not—" Her voice rose, and again she struck the table as she repeated the words,—" I will not go and beg pardon of the man who turned me out of my own room, and in the presence of a menial servant."

" Annabella, this is the excitement of fever ; you require—surely I hear Bardon's voice below ! " said the vicar, who found it impossible to manage his niece in her present mood, and who was almost alarmed at the wildness of her manner. " Would you see the doctor ? " added Mr. Aumerle.

Annabella hesitated for a moment, then exclaimed, " Dr. Bardon ! yes, I will see him at once." She remained in her standing position, rigid as a statue, till the vicar, after a brief absence, introduced the physician into the room, and then himself retired to another.

CHAPTER XIV.

A FATAL STEP.

"The arrow once discharged from this weak hand,
Can I arrest its flight in the free air?
Where will this course now lead me?"
                              CAMOENS.   BY H. S. G. TUCKER.

THE countess advanced one step towards Bardon,
and held out her hand. He took it cordially, and
looked at her bloodless face with mingled interest and
concern.

"Do not suppose," said Annabella, resuming her
seat, and motioning to him to take a chair beside her,
—"do not suppose that I see you in order to ask for
your medical advice. You must know well that it
is beyond your power to 'minister to a mind dis-
eased,' that my case is not one which the whole
pharmacopeia can cure. I see you as a friend,"—
her lip quivered as she spoke,—"as one who will
understand my feelings, and not torment me with
well-meant advice which I would rather die than
follow!"

"You are a noble creature—a brave creature!"
exclaimed Bardon; "I am proud of the spirit which
you have shown."

" Have you been far to-day ? " asked the countess, colouring slightly at the ill-merited praise.

" I was at Pelton this morning on business, or I should have called upon you earlier," was the doctor's reply.

" You have been, doubtless, at many houses," —Annabella seemed to frame each sentence with difficulty,—" you have seen many people—have heard—heard much that is—that must be said—and—." She stopped, and looked at the doctor, but he did not seem disposed to guess the meaning of her unfinished sentence.

" I wish to learn from you," continued the countess, forcing herself to a more explicit explanation ; " it is important for me to know what the world says of this—this unhappy affair."

" You care as little as I do for what the world says," replied the doctor.

But it was not so with Annabella. Popular distinction, the applause of others, had been to her as the breath of life. Her pride was not the pride of self-sufficiency ; she was intensely desirous to know whether public opinion were inclining to her side or that of her lord, and she pressed the doctor for a more definite reply.

" Of course," he answered at last, " there are almost as many versions of the story as there are narrators of it. No tale loses by the telling. Some say this thing, some say that, some pity, and some blame.

I

What is, however, pretty universally received as the most authentic account is— "

" Tell me !" cried the countess nervously, as the speaker paused.

" Why, it is said that you had somehow got into the snares of the Papists. That an old priest and a nun in disguise had made their way into Dashleigh Hall ; and, some affirm, had a private mass there. That the earl discovered amongst your papers a prayer to the Virgin, or something of that sort, and that he was so much disgusted by what he called your apostasy, that tearing the paper into a thousand fragments, he turned you out of the room."

" Did any one believe such a senseless tale ? " cried Annabella.

" It was said to come from the best authority, and is very generally credited."

" Did you not give it indignant refutation ? "

" My dear lady, you forget that I am in utter darkness upon the subject myself. I could stake my life that you had good cause for what you did, but of that cause I know no more than this chair."

" Then you shall know all," exclaimed Annabella, " that you may be able to give an answer to such idle calumnies as these ; " and with rapid utterance she gave the doctor an account of what had occurred, her narrative following truth in the main, though coloured by prejudice and passion.

Bardon's face showed gloomy satisfaction as he

listened to the excited speaker. "So then," he exclaimed as she concluded, "your crime is having drawn so faithful a portrait, that he who sat for it would not own it! What a fool he was to quarrel with one who has him so completely at her mercy!"

"What do you mean?" said Annabella quickly.

"You carried your desk with you, did you not?" said Bardon, with an expressive glance at that on the table; "and you carried with you the wit that can sting. Write out that paper again; give it to the public;—the world will laugh, and the earl will wince. No one who reads but will understand (I will do my best to enlighten dull comprehensions) *why* the peer was so angry with his wife—*why* he who stood trembling on the mountain was afraid of the wit of a woman."

"It would be retribution!" exclaimed Annabella.

"It would be revenge!" cried the haughty old man.

Little did the Aumerles divine that the physician whom they had admitted in order that he might quiet a fevered pulse, was pouring venom into a wound which he should rather have sought to heal; that he was doing the work, obeying the hest of the demon Pride, and drawing further from happiness and peace the young creature who had turned to him in her distress.

There was a strange, almost fierce satisfaction in the looks of Dr. Bardon when he descended to the

sitting-room, that was incomprehensible to the Aumerles.

" You will send her a sleeping draught ? " said the
vicar.

" I have given her something *to compose,*" replied
Bardon, a grim smile relaxing his features.

" You think her very feverish ? " inquired Ida.

" Oh, there's nothing to alarm," said the doctor ;
" she will be much relieved by-and-bye."

As soon as he had quited the vicarage, Ida went up
to Annabella's room, and gently knocked at the door.

" I wish to be alone !" said a voice from within,
and Ida immediately retired.

When the carriage which had been ordered by
Augustine Aumerle rolled up to the front of the
vicarage, Ida was sent again to try her powers of
persuasion, to induce the countess to avail herself of
it to return to her husband's home.

Ida felt the errand painful, and almost hopeless.
She hesitated for a moment ere she knocked, and
heard within the sound of a pen moving rapidly over
the paper.

"Annabella, my love," began Ida, as she softly unclosed the door.

The countess was bending over her desk, appa-
rently absorbed in writing. Her back was towards
the door, but she started on the entrance of Ida, and
turning hastily round showed a countenance crimsoned
to the temples with a burning flush.

"I can't be disturbed!" she exclaimed in a voice strangely harsh and impatient.

"O dear cousin!" cried Ida, "if you would but listen for a moment——"

"I will hear you to-morrow," said Annabella, "let me feel that in this room at least I am safe from unwelcome intrusion!"

Intrusion! what a word——and from those lips! Ida Aumerle was deeply hurt, not to say offended, and returned again to her family mortified and dejected. The vicar breathed a weary sigh, and Mrs. Aumerle said something about "a termagant," which made Mabel extremely angry.

"So then I must be off!" said Augustine. "I had so little hope of the fair lady's yielding, that, as you see, my travelling bag is all ready. Farewell, Mrs. Aumerle; thanks for your hospitality. Lawrence, remember that I expect you all at Aspendale on the 12th. I shall be glad if by that time you think my friend Mabel sufficiently fledged to try a flight in the blue empyrean!"

After her uncle's departure Ida retired with a heavy heart to the little room which, since Annabella's arrival, she had shared with her sister Mabel. The gratitude which a woman feels towards one who has offered to her his home and his heart, and the affection which Ida had from childhood entertained for her cousin, rendered both the earl and the countess objects of deep interest to the maiden. Family div-

ision jarred on her soul, like discord on a musical ear,
and Ida felt perhaps as forcibly as her stepmother
could, the evil of the course which Annabella was
wilfully pursuing.   She was wounded by the words
of impatience from her cousin, which sensitiveness
construed into actual unkindness, and Ida could
scarcely draw her thoughts sufficiently from the subject which engrossed them, to write a letter in reply
to some petition for relief which she knew that it
would be wrong to postpone.

Ida lingered over her letter till she began to fear
that it might be late for the post, to which she proposed taking it herself.   As she was putting on her
scarf, in preparation for her walk, Ida heard the
countess's bell, — Annabella was ringing for her
maid.   When Ida left her apartment she met the
attendant in the passage, on her return from the
room of the lady.

"Is the countess feeling unwell?" inquired Ida.

"Her ladyship only rang," replied Bates, "to
desire me to get ready to carry her letters to the
post."

"I am going thither myself," said Ida; "I will take
my cousin's notes; I think that you might be late."

"Thank you, miss," replied the maid; "but my
lady said expressly that I was to post the letters myself, and not let them out of my hand till I did so.
Perhaps I might carry yours also, Miss Aumerle; I
shall not be a minute in dressing."

Ida thanked the maid for the offer, and gave the note into her charge. But when Bates had hurried off to make her little preparations, Ida stood motionless in thought. Her heart misgave her as to the nature of the despatches which Annabella had evidently written with such nervous haste, and was about to send off with such anxious precaution. Why should the countess object to trust her letters to any one but her own menial servant? did she fear that the eye of a loving relative should chance to rest on the address? Was Annabella about to take some foolish step which should further alienate her from her husband? Ida remembered with pain the expression which she had last beheld on the countess's face.

"I had better go to her,—I may be in time to prevent some act which Annabella would hereafter bitterly regret." This was Ida's first thought, and under its impulse she almost laid her finger on the handle of her cousin's door. But another feeling made her pause and draw back. Had she not already found her presence regarded as an unwelcome intrusion,—should she subject herself again to repulse? "Back! back!" whispered Pride, though so softly that his tones were not recognised; "force not your society on one who doesnot desire it, your counsel on her who despises it."

Ida hesitated—went away some few steps, and then returned to the door, as if attracted towards her

unhappy cousin by some invisible spell. Again
there was a moment's reflection, again Pride recalled
to her mind her late discourteous reception by the
countess, and with a sigh of doubt and apprehension,
Ida Aumerle returned to her own room.

In the meantime Annabella with a trembling hand
had sealed up two large envelopes. The one contained "The Precipice and the Peer," hastily but
vigorously written, and was directed to the editor
of the magazine in which the countess had, as before
mentioned, occasionally written. The other letter
was addressed to her publisher in London, giving
him her free permission not only to complete the
printing of her romance, but to put the authoress's
name on the title-page, not as "Egeria," but " the
Countess of Dashleigh."

"I will show my lord," thought the proud, young
authoress, "that I can bring more dignity to the
name by my pen, than he by his sounding title. I
shall make him envy the renown of the woman whom
he thought it condescension to marry! He has thought
to humble—to subdue—to crush me ; I will prove
to him that I can stand alone, ay, stand on a loftier
pedestal than any to which he ever had power to
raise me! And *he* will be humbled, mortified! He
would not have the world even guess that his wife
could join the throng of authors, or touch a publisher's pay; he will see that his wife glories in the
talents which admit her among the aristocracy of

genius! I have now broken my chain, and can soar aloft unfettered!"

Thoughts like these animated the ambitious girl while actually engaged in her work. Intoxicated by anger and pride, she gave no audience to reason or conscience, but wrote as if writing for life. But when Annabella had actually placed the two letters in the hands of her maid, when she had heard the door close after Bates, there came a sudden revulsion of feeling, and the countess was startled and alarmed at what she herself had done. Was she not giving mortal offence to him whom she was bound to honour? could she expose him to ridicule without bringing deeper disgrace upon herself? Had not the church pronounced them to be one? Annabella's eye fell on the little circlet of gold which Reginald had placed on her finger on the solemn occasion when, in the sight of men, and the presence of God, she had taken him for her wedded husband, never to be divided from him, as she then hoped and believed, until death itself should them part! How many associations were linked with the sight of that ring! If gratified pride had powerfully inclined Annabella to incline to Reginald's suit, that pride had once been closely linked with love. She had once listened eagerly for his step, fondly gazed on his handwriting, heard the tones of his voice with delight, and believed her heart to be unalterably his! Annabella ran to her window which commanded a prospect of

the road which led to the village, with an undefined
yet strong wish to call back the messenger whom
she had sent. She saw Bates walking briskly from
the house, but yet so near, that her mistress's voice
might reach her. The countess called her, but faintly,
for a feeling of shame choked her voice. Bates did
not hear, did not stop. But the sound reached another ear, and Mabel, attired for a walk, came forth
from the house, and looked up to the window at
which the countess now stood. The young girl's
face was bright and kindly, and the light shining on
her blue eyes and auburn tresses, gave her, to the
fancy of her cousin, the appearance of pictured Hope.

" Did you wish to call back Bates ?" asked Mabel.
" I will run and being her back in a moment."

How important in life may be a single second,
when on its little point hangs a momentous decision !
The countess almost pronounced the word "yes!"
but with the rapidity of lightning, Pride poured his
suggestions into her ear. Not only would the revo-
cation of the order given appear weak indecision to
the maid, but Mabel would naturally carry back the
letters, while Bates proceeded to the post with Ida's,
and she could hardly avoid seeing their addresses. She
would then easily guess the cause of their writer's
vacillation and change of purpose ; she would conclude
that her cousin had penned that which she was afraid
or ashamed to send. These ideas took much less
time in rushing through the brain of Annabella, than

they have done in passing before the eye of the reader, and they silenced the assent which trembled on the lip of the irresolute countess.

"Shall I call back Bates?" asked Mabel again.

"No," answered Annabella from above; and retiring from the window the miserable girl threw herself on a chair, and exclaiming, "It is too late now, —too late! the irrevocable step is taken!" she covered her face with her hands, as if by so doing she could shut out reflection. Yet, strange to say, she yet clung to the shadow of a hope that Bates might find the post-office closed, and bring back to her the fatal letters!

CHAPTER XV.

THE DESERTED HOME.

"Thine honour is my life, both grow in one,
Take honour from me and my life is done!"
                                        SHAKSPEARE.

THE Earl of Dashleigh had suffered more acutely
from the departure of his wife, than Annabella or
the world believed. He missed her presence in his
home more painfully than even to himself he would
own. The nobleman was, as I have said, not of a
hard disposition, and by nature was of a sociable
temperament. Pride had indeed drawn around him
an icy barrier which greatly shut him out from
friendly intercourse with his neighbours, but this very
isolation made him the more dependent upon the few
with whom he could stoop to associate. Dashleigh
had scarcely been aware of how much pleasure he
had derived from his wife's wit and lively conversation, till he found himself suddenly thrown on his
own resources which were limited, and his own reflections which were unpleasant. He wandered
listlessly through his long suite of apartments; their
splendid decorations made them but appear to their

owner more empty, desolate, and dull. Yet Dashleigh dared not quit them for more cheerful scenes,
for he felt, with the instinctive shrinking of a shy,
proud, sensitive man, that his domestic concerns were
now the theme of a thousand tongues and that he
could appear in no place where he would not be an
object of observation and remark. Solitude was
hateful to the peer, but society would have been yet
more distasteful.

And Dashleigh was not satisfied with himself.
The words of Augustine Aumerle, pleading for an
inexperienced girl doing a foolish thing from a sudden
ebullition of temper, often recurred to the mind of
the husband. A thousand times the questions would
force themselves on his mind. " Have I not been
harsh to Annabella? might I not have overlooked a
fault? would not a little indulgence have touched
a warm heart like hers, and have made her destroy
with her own hand what she knew must have given
me offence? Was not the entrance of the duke at
that most unfortunate moment when I myself had
given way to passion, sufficient to irritate beyond all
power of self-control a woman—a wife—and a
peeress!" There was much of candour, much of
generosity in the spirit of Dashleigh, and so strong
did his self-reproach become, that the earl felt
greatly disposed to pass a sponge over the past, and
exchange mutual forgiveness with his wife. But
then the first advance must be on her side; Pride

peremptorily insisted on that. If Annabella were penitent, Reginald would be generous, but never would he degrade himself by suing for reconciliation, however fervently he might desire it.

Thus day passed after day, each more intolerable than the last, Reginald always hoping that the pride of his young partner might give way, and yearning for the supplicating letter which might give him an excuse for forgiving.

One morning, as the Earl of Dashleigh sat at his solitary breakfast, he listlessly took up the last number of the ——— Magazine, which the footman had, according to custom, placed beside the plate of his master. Light reading was that to which the earl could alone now bend his attention, and his thoughts often wandered as he glanced carelessly down the page. He was however instantly attracted by the name " Dashleigh" in capital letters on the sheet of advertisements, and read with a surprise which almost mastered even his indignation,—

Now in the press.
THE FAIRY LAKE: A Romance. By the COUNTESS OF DASHLEIGH.

" This is indeed throwing away the scabbard; this is indeed making a parade of insolent disregard of my wishes and commands! I hardly expected this from Annabella!" Such was the nobleman's muttered exclamation, as he pushed back his chair from the table. But his feelings received a far ruder shock

when he examined the periodical more closely. He
gazed on "The Precipice and the Peer," as it seemed
to glare upon him from the close-printed column, as
if he scarcely could believe the evidence of his senses!
Could it be,—yes—the initial and the dash could not
deceive him, could deceive no one who knew him!
Annabella had held him up to the ridicule of the
world, as a poor, nervous, spiritless wretch,—it was
revenge, mean, despicable revenge, a blow aimed at
the most vulnerable point!

The earl did not tear the periodical, and scatter its
fragments on the wind, he knew that it was spreading
at that hour through the halls and even cottages of
the land; that it was lying on the tradesman's
counter, in the servant's hall; that schoolboys were
laughing over the peer's adventure during the inter-
vals of more active sport! Dashleigh laid down the
magazine quietly, but with something resembling a
groan! Bardon had said that he would wince,—he
did more, he actually writhed under the torture inflicted by the hand of his wife!

The servants, wondering at the delay of the accustomed ring, came at length unsummoned, and bore
away the untasted breakfast. Dashleigh felt annoyed
at the jingling sound, but scarcely comprehended its
cause, and only experienced a sense of relief when
the room became silent again. His reflections were
bitter indeed; he was almost too wretched to be
angry. Was he not a disgraced, an insulted man?—

did not his very rank make him only a more promi-
nent mark for ridicule?   Could he ever show his face
again in circles which he had once deemed honoured
by his presence?   The time-darkened portraits of
deceased Earls of Dashleigh seemed to scowl down
from their heavy gilt frames on the first of the
name who had ever been branded with the imputa-
tion of fear!

A servant brought a letter on a salver; the earl
mechanically broke open the seal.   It was from the
vicar, Lawrence Aumerle, and had been written in
the first impulse of his indignant surprise on the appearance of the obnoxious article which he could not
doubt had been written by his niece.

The clergyman, with instinctive delicacy, avoided
all direct reference to the piece so indiscreetly com-
posed by Annabella; but he expressed the extreme
distress felt by both his family and himself at the
position in which she had placed herself.   He entreated her husband to believe that if he gave the
lady the protection of his home, it was not because
he sanctioned or even palliated her more than impru-
dent conduct, but that he feared that harshness might
drive her from a place where unceasing efforts were
made to bring her to a sense of her duty.

" Lawrence Aumerle is a good man," said the
earl, passing his hand across his brow, and leaning
thoughtfully back in his chair.   " Since all connexion
between me and her is broken now for ever—for ever,

better that the wretched girl should remain under
the protection of her mother's relations. It were
worse, far worse that her pride and folly should be
pampered by intercourse with the world,—that world
to which she has sacrificed her husband !"

Dashleigh arose and paced slowly the length of
the room, but returned with a more rapid step.
The name of Aumerle had suddenly suggested to
him a course by which he could fling from himself
the opprobrium which attaches to the name of a
coward. He grasped at the new idea with the
energy of a drowning wretch. The world should
have no cause to laugh at the man whose nerves had
failed him on the heights of a mountain ; he would
do that which should from henceforth effectually
silence such reproach. Taking up writing materials,
Dashleigh with rapid hand traced the following note
to Augustine :—

" DEAR AUMERLE,—You mentioned to me that a balloon is to
ascend from your grounds on the 12th. I should feel greatly
obliged by your reserving a place for me in the car, as it is my particular wish to make one in the excursion.—Ever yours,
                                                    " DASHLEIGH."

The brief note written and despatched to Aspendale, the nobleman breathed more freely. He could
meet the eye of his fellow-men. Pride rendered
the effort needful ; pride roused his spirit to make
it, and Dashleigh would not now pause to consider
how great that effort might be to one of his nervous

K

frame.   He felt that his honour was at stake.   The
earl was somewhat in the position of the knight of
old, whose lady flung her glove into the arena where
a fierce lion and tiger were contending, and before a
circle of noble spectators, bade him bring it back to
her hand.   The knight dreaded the laugh of the
audience more than the yells of the furious beasts,
and Dashleigh shrank from the sneer of the world
more than the untried perils of the air.   Annabella
had put her husband on his mettle ; she had incited
him to wrestle down nature ; but it remained to be
seen whether she had cause to triumph in the effect
produced by her satirical pen.

CHAPTER XVI.

PLEADING.

"Then be the question asked, the answer given,
As in the presence of the God of heaven;
All prejudice subdued, all pride laid low,—
'Whence have I come, and whither will I go?'
Whence have I come? what wandering steps have led
To this the painful desert that I tread?
From what neglected duties have I fled
Am I the sufferer from others' sin,
Or bear my most insidious foe within?
And whither would I go? where have I sought
Refuge from secret gloom and bitter thought?
Deep in the barren wilderness of pride?

Some crosses are from heaven sent,
And some we fashion of our own;
By envy, pride, and discontent
What thorns across our path are strown!
Not these the thorns that form the crown,
Not this the cross that lifts on high,—
Our sharpest trials we lay down
When sin and self we crucify!

"I OWN it, dear Ida, I own it! I did wrong, very wrong. I felt that as soon as the letter had passed from my hand; I must have been mad when I sent it. I wrote to the London editor the next day to endeavour to stop the publication, but the piece was already in type."

Such, after a painful conference, was the confession which conscience wrung from the Countess of Dashleigh.

Annabella was reclining on the sofa, her hair disordered, her eyes red with weeping. Ida was kneeling beside her, and the magazine lay on the floor.

" O Anna, Anna! why not own all this to your husband ; throw yourself on his mercy, entreat his forgiveness——"

" It would be of no use ! " exclaimed Annabella ; " that paper he never will forgive. I have already merited his anger ; I will not expose myself to his contempt."

" We may be objects of contempt when we wander from the line of duty, but never when we are struggling back to it again. When we are lost in a thorny labyrinth, what wiser, what nobler course can we pursue, than to retrace every step of the way ? "

" I can't, I can't," gasped Annabella; "there is now a deep gulf between me and my husband ! "

" Which is widening every moment ; which delay may render impassable ! It is yet spanned by a slender bridge of hope ; but that bridge is trembling, ——shaking,——Annabella, if you hold back now, it may sink before your eyes, and for ever ! "

" What would you have me to do ? " said the countess.

" Write a letter to the earl full of the humblest submission ; tell him with what real grief and con‑ trition——"

"Ida, you do not know me!" cried Annabella, pushing the loose hair impatiently back from her temples; "I cannot play the part of a penitent child, begging pardon for having been naughty; I cannot cringe beneath the rod, like a slave trembling before his master!"

"Anna!" exclaimed Ida, fixing on her cousin the earnest gaze of her expressive eyes, "must the slender bridge—your last hope—be broken down beneath the weight of your pride?"

"Pride," observed the Countess, " has been termed the weakness of noble natures."

"Pride,—what is it," exclaimed Ida, "as mirrored in the word of God? Is it not of *the world*,—that world that *passeth away;* doth not the Lord resist *the proud*, while giving *grace unto the humble?* Doth not inspired truth declare that *before destruction the heart of man is haughty, and before honour is humility?* Is not the Saviour's blessing on *the meek*, and on such as are *poor in spirit?* Why should I multiply quotations? Your own heart must tell you, dear Anna, that if one thing more than another stands between man and his Maker, and darkens the light of Heaven, it is the baneful spirit of pride!"

"It is interwoven with my nature," said the countess.

"The life-long battle of the Christian is with his fallen nature, but it is a struggle in which he is not

left alone.   Nay, *a new heart*, a new nature is given
to those who seek it in earnest prayer ; a new heart
filled with the Spirit of God, a new nature con-
formed to the likeness of Him who was *meek and
lowly* in spirit.   What are the Bible emblems of
those who are the soldiers and saints of the Lord ?
The lamb, the dove, the little child !   Can such be
fit types of one who struggles against lawful
authority, and recoils from the duty of submission ? "

Annabella was a little nettled.   " I think," she
observed, with some sarcasm in her tone, " that my
saintly cousin is not yet herself so perfect in this
virtue of submission, as to entitle her so eloquently
to enforce it on another."

Ida glanced up in surprise.   She had not been
aware that the quick observation of her cousin had
detected in her the lurking enemy of whose presence
she herself was scarcely aware, and against whom
she was hardly on her guard.   But she could not
deny the truth of the accusation so suddenly brought
against her, and was too earnest in the cause which
she was advocating to be silenced by a personal
remark.

" Oh! my dear cousin !" she replied, her soft, dark
eyes filling with tears, " let not my errors be a
stumbling-block in the way of those whom I love.
Look not at the miserable transcript, all stained and
blotted with human infirmity, but turn your eyes to

the blessed Original which is set before us, that we
may copy its sacred features into our hearts and our
lives! What was the spirit of Christ? and hath
not Truth declared that *if any man hath not the
Spirit of Christ he is none of His?* Was it not a
spirit patient under suffering, meek under insult, a
spirit ever ready to forgive? Did He not love his
enemies, bless them that cursed Him, and do good to
them that persecuted Him? Look on Him, dearest,
look on Him, till in the brightness of His glory sin
appear all the darker and more hateful! There is
no pride in heaven, Annabella; we must throw away
the chain ere we reach that bright place, or we
never can enter therein! It is pride that is now
shutting you out of your earthly home, barring
against you a husband's heart, changing domestic
peace to misery. Oh, how terrible the thought
that pride has shut out multitudes from an eternal
home, made them aliens from a heavenly Father,
rendered them sharers in the fate of that terrible
being, who lost a seraph's crown through his pride!
God grant,—God grant that neither you nor I may
ever be reckoned amongst them!"

The voice of Ida trembled with emotion, the large
tears coursed down her cheeks, and her hands were
tight-clasped as if in earnest supplication. It was a
sister imploring a sister in danger to seek safety
while safety might be found, to tear from her heart
the coiling serpent that was lurking there only to

destroy!   Annabella could not be angry; she was
touched by that pleading look; the ice was beginning
to thaw, and yet was too strong readily to give way.
What was she called upon to do ?   Not only to forgive, but to entreat for forgiveness, to humble herself
in the dust before him to whom her proud spirit
had never yet learned to bow !   The countess felt
that it would be hardly possible so to stoop,—that
even for heaven itself she could scarcely sacrifice
that which it would be hard to part with, even as a
right hand or a right eye !   The momentary struggle
was fearful !   Wringing her hands, Annabella exclaimed, " O Ida, you know not how wretched you
make me !"

"And who deserves to be wretched," said Mrs.
Aumerle, who happened at this time to enter the
room, "if not she who chooses no guide but her
own temper and caprice, who will listen to no advice
—not even that of her uncle and her pastor, and
who publicly insults the husband whom she is bound
in duty to honour ?   Rise, Ida, rise," continued the
lady, to whose plain sense of right and wrong Annabella's conduct appeared unpardonable; " I am
ashamed to see you on your knees beside a girl who,
if she were fifty times a countess, has forfeited claim
to our respect."

Annabella sprang from her sofa, and with eyes
wide open and lips apart, stood listening, as her
hostess, to Ida's distress and dismay, finished her

rebuke to one whom she regarded as a spoiled, self-willed, obstinate child.

"There is only one excuse for you, Anna, and that is to be found in the indulgence and flattery to which you have been accustomed from the cradle. You have been unfitted to take your proper place either as a wife or the mistress of a household. You have made everything subservient to your humour. But it is time to have done with such childish follies; it is time to renounce the petulant pride which makes your family blush for you! Mr. Aumerle is so indulgent, so unwilling to treat any one harshly, that you are hardly aware, I suspect, how strongly he feels on the subject; but I can assure you that he views your late step in the same light as I do, and he has written to the earl to express to him his strong disapprobation of your conduct."

"Has he!" exclaimed the countess almost fiercely "then this house is no longer a place for me! I have stayed here too long already!" and stretching out her hand to the bell-rope, she pulled it violently to summon her maid. "I have been driven out of one home by unkindness, I will not remain in another to be insulted by such language as you have dared to address to me!" Again, with the force of passion, Annabella rang the bell, and it was answered, not only by Bates but by Mabel, who ran in alarmed by the second loud ring, and the sound of a voice raised in anger.

"Bates," cried the countess, "bring me what I
may require for walking, and then pack up my
boxes, and follow me as soon as possible to the
cottage in which Dr. Bardon resides."

"But—my lady—"

"At once!" cried the impatient countess.

"O Annabella, dearest Annabella, do not leave
us!" exclaimed Mabel, clinging to her cousin, while
Ida, almost too much agitated to be intelligible,
joined her entreaties to those of her sister.

"Wait—if it were only one day—one hour—only
till papa should return!"

But Annabella was inexorable. She had worked
herself into that state of passion in which remonstrance seems to have no effect but that of adding
fuel to the flame. The storm of anger was less
intolerable to her spirit than the state of doubt and
self-reproach, which, like a chill, dark mist was
falling on her soul, when the words of Mrs. Aumerle
roused her from remorse to sudden resentment. The
countess determined to seek the dwelling of Bardon,
where she felt assured of a welcome, and where she
would remain, as she declared, till she had formed
arrangements with friends in London. It was, perhaps, unfortunate that Annabella had sufficient
resources of her own to render her in pecuniary concerns quite independent of others. She had just
arrived at the age which gave her free disposal of
these resources, though it had certainly not proved,

in her case, to be an age of discretion. It was fore-
seeing the difficulties and dangers that must beset
the wealthy and wilful girl, whose vanity would
render her the ready dupe of interested flatterers,
that had made the vicar anxious to keep her beside
him, until the kindly offices of mutual friends should
re-unite her to her husband. This was now impossible. Annabella, closing her ears to remonstrance,
and her heart to tenderness, quitted the home of her
uncle with an expressed determination never to
revisit it again. She would not even suffer her
cousins to accompany her, but with sullen resolution
set out on her lonely walk.

Ida watched her receding figure with a very heavy
heart. "It might have been so different," she murmured to herself; "her heart was touched, her pride
was giving way, when—" and turning towards the
spot where her step-mother stood, Ida could not
refrain from the exclamation, "it was your coming
that changed all!", Without lingering for a reply
to the hastily spoken word, Ida sought solitude in
the quiet arbour where she had, as we have seen,
held converse with her sister upon subjects high and
holy. Ida's only companions now were bitter meditations. She had reproached her father's wife, but
was her own conscience clear even as regarded Annabella? Ida recalled with deep distress her own mis-
givings on the day on which the countess must have
written her fatal paper.

"If I had only spoken to her then,—if I had
only pleaded with her then, before the irrevocable
step had been taken, oh! it would never have come
to this!" and with the anguish of unavailing regret,
Ida Aumerle mourned over her sin of omission.

CHAPTER XVII.

CONSCIENCE ASLEEP.

"Those, however, who having no such plea to urge, are envious, sour, discontented, irritable, uncharitable, have good ground to suspect the genuineness of their Christianity. Grace sweetens while it sanctifies."—GUTHRIE.

How wide a difference do we find to exist between
the consciences of those who hold the same faith,
and profess to be governed by the same command-
ments! To some—sin appears like the speck on a
bridal robe, a disfiguring blot seen at a glance, which
offends the eye, and to remove which every means
at once must be taken. To others—it is a thing as
little to be marked as the same speck on a dark,
time-worn garment. The possessor wears it with
an easy mind, perhaps all unconscious of the stain!

Thus while Ida grieved at the recollection of that
false delicacy or hidden pride, that had made her
shrink from intruding herself upon her cousin at a
time when her presence might have been of essential
service, Bardon felt not the least self-reproach for
the evil counsel which he had given to the countess.
It was to him merely a subject of pleasant specula-
tion whether she would follow it or not, and he

was extremely impatient for the day when the
appearance of the next number of the ——— Magazine
would set all his doubts to rest. Bardon longed to
see a good home-thrust at the pride of Reginald,
Earl of Dashleigh. The mortification of the peer—
his confusion—his indignation—was a subject upon
which the imagination of the doctor actually feasted,
for he had never forgotten or forgiven the words
that he had overheard at the Hall.

And yet Bardon was not considered a bad man,
nor was he such as the word is commonly understood. He was an honest, upright man; a steady
friend, an earnest patriot, one who felt for the suffer-
ings of the poor, though he had little power to
relieve them. And Bardon was to a certain extent
religious, at least in his own opinion. He read and
venerated his Bible, constantly attended his church,
and had persecution arisen, would have been a
martyr of the cause of truth.

But Bardon's religion did not pervade his spirit,
it did not leaven his temper. It left him as jealous,
irritable, and vindictive, as if he had never heard of
a gospel of peace!

> " In yonder vase replenished by the shower
>   Pour the rich wine; it spreads as it descends,
> Pervades the whole, and with mysterious power
>   To every drop its hue and sweetness lends!
> Thus should religion's influence serene
> Be felt in all our thoughts, in all our actions seen!"

But it was not thus with Timon Bardon. He could
repeat the Lord's prayer,—did repeat it twice every

day, without once starting at the thought, that he
was in it constantly invoking a curse on his own
vindictive soul! Forgive us our trespasses, *as we
forgive them that trespass against us!* Was that a
prayer for one who treasured up the memory of a
wrong far more jealously than that of a benefit? for
one who prided himself on being "a good hater;"
and who spoke of "the sweetness of revenge?"
Bardon reprobated with indignation the mean vices
of covetousness, falsehood, or fraud,—he was ready
to call down fire from heaven on the tyrant, the
traitor, or the thief; but he granted, in his own
person, a plenary indulgence, a perfect tolerance to
pride, hatred, malice, revenge—sins as destructive
to the soul as the darkest of those which he condemned.

Bardon was too poor to be a subscriber to the
—— Magazine; but he was always allowed a
reading of that which was taken in at the Vicarage,
and, indeed, Aumerle, though his friend little guessed
the fact, subscribed chiefly on account of the doctor.
But Bardon was far too impatient to know whether
the countess had written in this Number, to endure
waiting for a second day's reading. He did not
choose to go to the Vicarage to betray his eagerness
there, but he resolved to walk the whole six
miles to Pelton, in order to purchase a copy for
himself.

"You must have pressing business indeed at the

town, papa, to walk so far in the sun on such a warm
day as this !" cried Cecilia in a tone of expostula-
tion, as she fanned herself with a languid air.   " I'm
sure that the heat will kill you."

"Not so easily killed," said the doctor gaily ;
" there's nothing like air and exercise for keeping a
man in health."

"You have received a call to some patient ?" said
Cecilia, encouraged by his cheerfulness to venture
upon a subject which was usually forbidden, for
Bardon's patients were " few and far between."

"There's one who won't prove patient, I guess,"
replied Bardon inwardly chuckling at the joke.

His mind was so full of his errand that, though
the road was extremely dusty, and the sun shot down
fervid rays, Bardon was scarcely conscious either of
discomfort or fatigue.   He walked on as briskly as
if the frost of December braced his nerves and
rendered rapid motion necessary.   Bardon was glad,
however, when his journey drew near its end, and
he reached the High Street of Pelton, with its rows
of tidy shops, to one of which—the library—he now
bent his eager steps.   He glanced rapidly over the
window in hopes to recognise the well-known cover
of the ——— Magazine amongst prints, envelopes,
and daily papers ; it was not, however, to be seen,
and Bardon entered the library.

There was at first no one sufficiently disengaged
to be able to attend to the doctor, and Bardon had

to wait with what patience he could muster, taking off his hat, and wiping his heated forehead, and looking around him, but in vain, for the Number which he had walked so far to see.

"Warm morning, sir," said the librarian, turning to the doctor at last, as a party of customers quitted the shop.

"The last Number of the ——— Magazine!" cried Bardon, waving superfluous comment on the weather, and flinging down a coin on the counter.

"Well, sir," said the shopkeeper with a smile, "if you had called but five minutes ago I could have accommodated you with a copy; but there's been such a run on the Magazine to-day, that really I have not one left. You see, sir," he added, "there's an article in it that takes with the public amazingly,— something that's said to be a hit on one of the leading men in the county; and," here he lowered his voice, "people who are wiser than their neighbours think that they've a pretty good guess as to the pen that wrote it. Anything else this morning, sir?"

Bardon uttered his emphatic "No!" and hurried out of the shop. "She's done it!" he muttered to himself; "I'd give anything to see her paper!"

L

CHAPTER XVIII.

THE MAGAZINE.

"We must have satire, pungent, biting satire;
Such is the vile condition of our nature,
Such our depraved and vicious appetites,
No other food will suit our palsied taste."
CAMOENS, BY H. S. G. TUCKER.

AT the corner of the street a baker's boy and a gentleman's page were standing together, laughing at
something which the latter held in his hand, and
which his companion was perusing over his shoulder.

"Now, ain't that good?" exclaimed he of the
bread-basket, showing his teeth from ear to ear.

Bardon caught a glimpse of what they were reading. "My lads," he cried, "I'll pay you for that;
give the magazine to me," and he held out the price
for the Number.

"It's my master's," said the page, as if awakened
to a sudden sense of the responsibility connected
with green cloth and gilt buttons; and rolling up the
coveted Number, he hurried on his way to make up
for the time which he had lost.

The doctor stopped and reflected. "Mrs. Clayton, the major's blind widow, she is likely to take

in the —— Magazine. I have not called on the old dame for years, but she'll not take a visit amiss. I think that the house with green blinds is hers, and I am certain to find her at home."

Dr. Bardon was not disappointed this time. The blind old lady, who lived a dull and solitary life, was charmed to welcome an old acquaintance, and her visitor was yet more pleased to behold the desired periodical on the table half covered by the supplement of yesterday's *Times*.

After the first greetings were over, and inquiries after his "sweet child Caroline," (for the lady's memory was not particularly clear as to the name or age of Cecilia,) the doctor seated himself by the blind lady, laughing loud to cover the rustle as he drew the Magazine from under the paper, and then impatiently turned over the leaves. His object was to read the article; Mrs. Clayton's was to obtain a medical opinion gratis upon the maladies with which she was, or fancied herself to be troubled. She proceeded, therefore, quite uninterrupted by her supposed auditor, with a long story of rheumatism and relaxed throat, the various remedies which she had tried for these evils, and the dubious success of each application; the eager reader giving an occasional grunt of assent, to save appearances, until the invalid paused in her narration.

"Indeed, doctor, I'm beginning to think that the air of Pelton don't agree with me; I begin to feel myself—"

"Hanging between earth and sky, like the fabled coffin of Mahomet!" muttered the doctor, who in his interest in what he was perusing, had almost forgotten the presence of her whose faint, complaining voice sounded like a trickling rill in his ear.

"What is he saying about coffins and hanging?" thought the poor invalid. "It is very shocking to suggest such horrible ideas to a nervous creature like me!"

As the doctor did not seem disposed to add to his incomprehensible communication, Mrs. Clayton proceeded on with her melancholy story.

"Last winter my cough was so bad, that Mrs. Graham (you know Mrs. Graham, her daughter married a Bagot), she recommended me to take cochlico lozenges. I sent up all the way to London, there's only one shop there that sells them, in one particular street, and I got a parcel of them down by the post. But I assure you, doctor, that they did me no good. I think that I must have caught a chill by venturing out in March; you know what the east winds are, doctor; I really had not a wink of sleep at night,—I actually thought my cough would have torn me to pieces."

At this point the reader burst into an irrepressible chuckle of delight, and as he closed the Magazine exclaimed, "Capital! capital!" to the no small amazement of the sufferer. Her lengthened silence of surprise made Bardon,—whose hand was now on the supplement of the *Times*, aware that it was necessary to say something ; and as he had a vague idea that her talk had been a series of complaints, he cried, hap-hazard, as his eye ran on the list of deaths, " Very bad! very bad! I'm certain that you indulge in green tea !"—

" Oh ! well, I sometimes—"

" Can it be !" muttered Bardon, gazing with stern interest at one of the names which appeared in the gloomy column.

" Do you think, doctor, that there is much harm ?"

" Death !" exclaimed Timon Bardon to himself.

" Surely you don't mean it,"—cried the old lady, and the doctor was again recalled by her voice to what was passing around him.

"If you drink green tea," he cried, starting from his seat and pushing the paper to the other end of the table, " I won't answer for your living out the year !" and with a very brief good-bye, Timon hurried away, leaving the poor lady to complain to her next visitor, that Dr. Bardon was so brusque and so odd that he was just like an east wind in March, and that she was not in the least surprised that his practice was not extensive, as if he did not kill his patients with his medicine, he was likely to do so with his manner !

What was it that Bardon had seen in the *Times*

that interested him as strongly as even the article written by Annabella at his own suggestion? He had seen the announcement of the death of " Mr. Auger, of —— Street and Nettleby Tower," of the man who had ruined his prospects—who had wrested from the disinherited son the estate which his ancestors for centuries had held. Death should still the emotion of hatred, hush the voice of revenge; but it is to be feared that in this instance the advertisement, casually seen, rather increased than diminished the stern satisfaction felt by the vindictive old man. It seemed to Bardon as if he were triumphing at once over a dead and a living foe. As he proceeded on his long walk homewards, he certainly never questioned himself as to his lack of the charity which *rejoiceth not in iniquity*, or he would not have revelled as he did in the idea that it was he who had incited the countess to take such petty revenge on her husband. Nor did Bardon, as he reflected on the death of his hated supplanter, recall to mind the warning of the royal Preacher, *Rejoice not when thine enemy falleth, and let not thy heart be glad when he stumbleth*, or he would scarcely have muttered to himself with a gloomy smile, that six feet of earth would be now estate large enough for the late owner of Nettleby Tower.

Notwithstanding the engrossing nature of his thoughts, the doctor on his return to his home could not avoid feeling the way long and the weather oppressive. He could scarcely drag on his weary limbs when at length he reached the little gate of the garden which surrounded Mill Cottage.

Cecilia ran out to meet him in a flutter of excitement and joy.

"O! Papa! only guess who has come here while you were away!"

"How can I tell!" said the tired man sharply.

"The countess! the dear delightful countess herself, and she says——" but Doctor Bardon waited to hear no more, and forgetful of fatigue, hurried into the cottage.

Annabella came forward to meet him, and in a few brief sentences explained to him her situation, and her wish to remain no longer under the roof of her uncle the vicar. As she had expected, the doctor gave her a cordial welcome, and pressed her to remain at his home for as long a period as might suit her convenience. He was proud to be able to exercise hospitality, and though he would never have pleaded guilty to the charge, was by no means insensible to the honour of entertaining a woman distinguished both by her rank and her talents. Would it not also be an additional mortification to the detested earl, to know that the Countess of Dashleigh was the guest at a cottage scarcely larger than his gamekeeper's lodge!

As for Cecilia, she was in ecstasies. The presence of a real countess seemed to her actually to glorify

the little abode, and her only misery was the difficulty of providing suitable accommodation for such an
illustrious visitor. The cottage she had often termed
" nothing but a bandbox," and though poor Miss
Bardon was willing to put herself into any straits,
empty out all her drawers, squeeze herself and her
wardrobe into any corner, it required a wonderful
amount of ingenuity to make the titled guest and
her maid tolerably comfortable in the tiny tenement.
Cecilia not only used every effort to stimulate to
exertion her old deaf domestic, but herself worked
hard in secret to prepare her own room for the
countess. She ruthlessly sacrificed a white muslin
robe for the adornment of the toilette table, cut up
her best bow to loop it up with ribbon, and even
ventured to invade her father's garden to ornament
the apartment with flowers.

Annabella had little idea of the amount of trouble
and excitement which she was causing, nor how
heavily the expense of hospitality would press on
her proud but poor entertainers. While the countess was conversing in the sitting room with the
doctor, Bates arrived with her lady's boxes, and was
ordered to carry them up to her apartment. The
maid surprised poor Cecilia on her knees, indus-
triously stitching up a hole in a worn-out drugget,
her face flushed and heated with the unwonted occupation. Miss Bardon started up in some confusion,
her pride deeply mortified at being found in a position,

and engaged in an employment so unbefitting a
fine lady, which it was her ambition always to appear.

Bates looked round with wondering contempt on
the miserable hovel, as she deemed it, which her
young mistress had chosen in preference to the
luxurious apartments of Dashleigh Hall. The lady's
maid had serious doubts as to whether she could so
compromise her own dignity as to remain in a house
where no "footman was kept." To share a pigeon-
hole seven feet square with a deaf and stupid maid-
of-all-work, who could not even listen to her
gossip,—did ever devoted lady's maid submit to such
hardship before! Annabella, on her part, found
fault with nothing, never appeared to notice any
difficulties, and accommodated herself to cottage life
as if she had been accustomed to it from her childhood.

"There is not a particle of pride in her!" exclaimed the admiring Cecilia, as she had done upon a
previous occasion.

CHAPTER XIX.

EXPECTATION.

"It is you
Hath blown this coal betwixt my lord and me."

SHAKSPEARE.

THE announcement that our sovereign Lady herself
had resolved to take a bird's-eye view of her dominions
from the clouds, could hardly have created a greater
sensation in the county of Somersetshire, than the
rumour, presently confirmed " by authority," that the
Earl of Dashleigh was to be one of the aerial travellers
in the *Eaglet.* From the squire to the swineherd,
every one within a circuit of many miles was full of
the strange report. The nobleman's motive for attempting the feat was palpable to all who had read
or heard of " The Precipice and the Peer;" and specu-
lation was rife, and heavy bets were exchanged as to
whether the hero of the Swiss adventure would ever
summon up sufficient courage to mount aloft in a
balloon.

The rumour reached the dwelling of the Bardons.
The doctor elevated his bushy black brows, and drew
in his lips as if to whistle; while Cecilia stole a
glance at the countess to see the effect of the an-

nouncement upon her. Annabella changed colour, but affected to believe the report absurd, and dismissed the subject at once from her discourse if not from her thoughts. But from that hour the young wife's manner became reserved and gloomy. She made no effort to keep up conversation, did not seem to hear questions addressed to her, or if she heard, gave her replies at random. She would scarcely touch at table the delicate food procured for her with trouble and expense. Cecilia in vain taxed her brain to find something that a peeress could eat, and the doctor brought vegetables from his garden which he believed that Covent Garden could not equal, to see them lie untasted on the plate of his silent guest.

Under any other circumstances the temper of the old lion would have given way, but the report of Dashleigh's intended exploit had filled him with malignant delight. Bardon felt assured that the spirit of the adventurous peer would fail him when put to the proof, and so eager was the doctor to enjoy this expected new source of humiliation to his foe, that he resolved to accept Augustine's invitation after all, and make one of the spectators who should witness the ascent of the *Eaglet*.

Poor Cecilia, however, who had no such secret source of satisfaction,—who would, of course, be constrained to remain at home with her guest, and see nothing of the gaiety at Aspendale, began to suspect that even the honour of entertaining a peeress might

be purchased at too high a price. Annabella now
took no pains to flatter the little vanity of her
hostess; never even glanced admiringly at her elabo-
rate dress, never asked her to touch the guitar, praised
nothing, smiled at nothing, seemed really to care for
nothing; while the poor lady of the cottage scarcely
dared to think what her father would say when the
tradesmen should send in their formidable bills!

Amongst those who were most startled by the
news that Dashleigh had decided on ascending with
his friend, was the aspirant to the same perilous distinction, the enthusiastic Mabel Aumerle.   The warm
champion of the wife doubted at first whether she
could consistently make one in a party in which the
tyrant husband was to appear.   But Mabel did not
long waver in doubt. Her desire to share her uncle's
excursion was too intense to be easily damped.

"I need have nothing to say to the earl," she
observed, "even if sitting in the car by his side.
My uncle has a right to invite whom he pleases, and
I have none to find fault with his selection. Besides,
I daresay when it comes to the point, that the nervous earl will find some excuse for not ascending at
all."

Mabel might have added that late events had
shown her that her admired countess had not the
right altogether on her side.   With all her spirit of
partisanship, Mabel could not defend "The Precipice
and the Peer," and she was hurt and almost offended

at the abrupt manner in which her cousin had quitted
the vicarage. On the whole, therefore, Mabel decided that no reason existed to prevent her doing her
utmost to persuade her indulgent father to permit
her to join the æronauts in their excursion through
the realms of air.

The vicar and his wife, on hearing of the earl's
intention to be at Aspendale, at once relinquished
their purpose of going thither themselves. They
felt that there would be an awkwardness in meeting
him in society after receiving his disobedient young
wife into their house. Ida, also, for more than one
reason, declined her uncle's invitation. But to Mabel
staying away upon such an occasion would have been
a disappointment which the whole amount of her
philosophy would not have enabled her to bear; and
Augustine therefore arranged to drive over for his
youngest niece early on the morning of the eventful
12th of May.

"Ida, dearest," exclaimed Mabel on the evening
preceding the long-desired day, "do you know that
at last, after coaxing,—such hard, such persevering
coaxing,—I have really managed to get a sort of
consent from Papa to my going up in the *Eaglet!* I
took his arm as he was walking up and down upon
the lawn, and I was so persuasive, so irresistible, I
told him so much about Mr. Verdon, and how he
could manage a balloon just as easily as I manage a
pony,—that at last convinced——"

"Or tired out," suggested Ida,—

"He said to me, with his dear kind smile, 'I don't forbid your going, my child, but you must ask your mother's opinion about it.' O Ida! I could have danced for joy! What a kiss I gave him for the permission! There never was so kind a father as he!"

"But you had a condition to fulfil," observed Ida, "which must have moderated your delight."

"Yes; I am not fond of asking any one's opinion, above all, that of—well, don't look so grave, dear Mentor, I won't say anything to shock you; but to think of Papa's calling her my *mother!* Off I flew to Mrs. Aumerle, eager as a bird on the wing. I found her in her store-room, measuring out tea and sugar, soap and candles. 'Mrs. Aumerle,' I cried, without waiting to get my breath, 'Papa does not forbid my going up in the car of the *Eaglet* with my uncle, but he desires me to ask your—' The old horror did not even give me time to finish my sentence. 'Mabel,' she said, looking as prim as that poker, 'once for all, I tell you I will never give my consent to your doing so ridiculous a thing;' but she was overshooting her mark," continued Mabel, laughing gaily, "papa told me to ask her *opinion,* and not her *consent,*—there's a mighty difference between the two."

"But, Mabel, when Mrs. Aumerle positively forbids you to go—"

"She's not my mother!" cried Mabel quickly;

"I'm not bound to yield obedience to her. You do not do so yourself. Did not Mrs. Aumerle tell you to have nothing more to do with the woman at the toll, and yet you gave her some tea and warm flannel the very next day!"

"But, Mabel, I thought that the woman was misjudged and hardly treated, and—"

"She turned out to be a hypocrite, you know; but that is nothing to the point. The question is,—Whether you and I are to be lorded over by Mrs. Aumerle? whether we are forced to obey any one but our own dear father?"

Ida knew not what to reply; for had she counselled strict obedience to her step-mother, she too well knew that her practice would contradict her preaching.

"Ah! you think just as I do," cried Mabel; "we ought to be civil and attentive to Mrs. Aumerle for the sake of peace, and to please Papa, but we need not be ruled by her commands."

"In the present case," said Ida, avoiding the point of discussion, "I think that our step-mother may be right. I should not be easy if you were to be exposed to the slightest danger."

"Danger! nonsense!" cried Mabel; "when this is Mr. Verdon's fifteenth ascent, and we are to come down in a couple of hours! Why, even the earl, with his sensitive nerves, does not fear to ascend!"

"And yet I cannot help dreading—"

"Ida, Ida," exclaimed Mabel, putting her hand playfully before the lips of her sister, "you have no voice in the matter; Papa never told me to ask your consent or even your opinion. If he see no danger, why should you? You would never be so unkind, so dreadfully unkind, as to prevent my having what would be to me the greatest enjoyment in the world!"

Mabel said a great deal more which it is not necessary here to repeat, to remove every lingering objection which might be felt by her sister. Ida disliked the idea of the excursion, though half convinced by Mabel's arguments that there was no real cause for apprehension; but in her opposition she did not take her stand on the only tenable ground, —that of the duty of submission to lawful authority. Ida, with all her gentleness and tenderness of conscience, felt as strong a repugnance as her sister to bowing to the judgment of the woman to whom her sympathies so little inclined. She constantly repeated to herself that their natures and their spheres were different, and that the step-mother and step-daughters might each pursue their own course of usefulness without interfering with one another. Ida would be on the footing rather of a friendly ally than that of a dependent subject of the mistress of her father's house. Pride had not lost his hold upon the gentle, self-sacrificing Christian.

Mabel was very glad that during the evening the conversation of the family circle turned rather upon

Annabella and her husband than on her own share in the morrow's balloon expedition; she was so fearful lest anything should be said to induce her father to revoke his extorted permission to her to ascend in the car.

When the young ladies had retired for the night, the vicar said to his wife, "Did Mabel ask your consent, my dear, to the excursion on which her heart is so greatly set?" (the father, it may be observed, did not draw the nice distinction upon which Mabel had insisted between opinion and consent.)

"She did," replied the lady, folding up her work, "and I put an extinguisher at once upon the project."

"You did?" said the vicar thoughtfully; "well, I daresay, my love, you were right."

CHAPTER XX.

A SUNNY MORN.

> " Ay, those were days when life had wings,
>   And flew—ah! flew so wild a height,
> That like the lark that sunward springs,
>   I was giddy with too much light ! "
>
> MOORE.

IT was with a sensation of delightful expectation
that Mabel Aumerle rose on the following morning.
The sun rising over the distant hills was scarcely so
early as she. Mabel could hardly believe that the
long-expected day was actually come, on which her
most delightful dream of hope was to be fully
realized !

No one else in the vicarage was stirring when the
young girl crept softly from the house, for her spirit
felt so blythe and elastic that it could only expand in
freedom under the open vault of heaven. How
deliciously fresh was the breath of morn ! Mabel
gazed at the light clouds above her, and almost
shouted for joy at the thought that in a few hours
she would be winging her way amongst them, no
more chained down as a captive to earth. She would
no longer envy the little bird, pouring his carol down
from the sky—she would soar yet higher than he!

Mabel lingered about the garden for nearly two hours, too much excited to settle for a moment to any quiet occupation. She was troubled by nothing but the fever of impatience, and the fear that something might occur to stop her expected treat. She ever and anon looked anxiously towards the house; as long as Mrs. Aumerle's shutters were closed, Mabel retained a feeling of security; but as soon as she saw them open, the eager girl determined to go a little way on the road by which her uncle was to come, "to meet him and prevent delay," as she said to hesrelf, but really to give opportunity to no one to object to her ascent in the *Eaglet*.

How quiet the road appeared! how thick lay the diamond dew on the sward that fringed it! how bright and cheerful all nature looked to the rejoicing eye of Mabel! Yet her uncle seemed to her to take a wearisome time in coming. The minutes were terribly long, and the impatient girl could scarcely believe the testimony of the village church clock when it struck only the number eight.

"I think that the morning will never end!" exclaimed Mabel; "I was foolish to rise so early. But see,—see,—surely there is a gig coming at last down the hill,—and that is my uncle driving; I should know Black Prince miles off, he trots down at so dashing a pace! O uncle!" she cried, running forward to meet him, "it seemed as if you never would come!"

"I'm not late," said Augustine, reining up his horse, whose black hide was flecked with foam; "we shall be back in good time for breakfast. Up with you!" and Mabel, with eager pleasure, mounted to the seat at his side.

"Shall I just wish them good morning at the vicarage, and see if Ida has changed her mind?

"Oh no! pray don't," said Mabel uneasily, "I am certain that Ida would not come."

"Well, then, we had better be off for Aspendale, and not keep Verdon waiting for breakfast," cried Augustine, backing his horse up to the hedge to turn his head round on the narrow road.

"How good you are to come all this way for me!" said Mabel. "And so Mr. Verdon has really arrived; and the balloon, is it all right—all ready?"

"It will be ready by the time that our guests arrive," replied her uncle, lightly shaking the rein, and touching his steed with the whip, "Have you leave to ascend with us, Mabel?"

"Yes; Papa's leave, at least," she replied. "Oh! how delightful it is to go driving on at this pace; but it will be far more delightful still to go scudding aloft before the breeze!"

"Is not that Bardon's cottage?" asked Augustine, as they dashed past a little tenement. Mabel gave an affirmative reply.

"I had had some thought," observed her uncle, "of calling for Dr. Bardon; but I confess that, after what has past, I feel somewhat disgusted at his coming at all. There is a singular want of good taste in his showing himself at this time to Dashleigh."

"Surely the doctor is not going in the balloon!" exclaimed Mabel.

"No, no, not quite so bad as that," answered Augustine with a smile; "I could not undertake to carry up lion and bear in one car, even with my fair niece to help me to keep the peace between them."

"But do you believe," asked Mabel, "that the earl will really ascend?"

Augustine's handsome countenance became grave. "He must do something, poor fellow," he observed, "to efface from the minds of men the remembrance of that mischievous squib."

"But if he be really so timid—"

"Reginald has no want of courage," said Augustine Aumerle, with unusual warmth in his manner; "I have seen him plunge into a rapid stream to save a drowning child; and when we were boys together, I have known him fight a bully who was twice as strong as himself. Certainly he never could climb a tree," added the friend in a more thoughtful tone.

"And he played a poor figure on the mountain, according to 'The Precipice and the Peer,'" said Mabel.

"There was a great deal of exaggeration in that piece; any one could see that," replied Augustine.

" It contained the very essence of malicious satire. I don't know what could have possessed the countess to write it."

" Pride, I suppose," answered Mabel.

" Detestable pride!" muttered her uncle.

" But do you not think that they will be one day reconciled to each other? Annabella has so much that is noble in her ; she is so generous and affectionate,—and you seem to have a good opinion of the earl."

" The mischief is," replied Augustine, " that he is as proud as she. No, I fear that neither will ever yield, and that this grievous separation will last as long as their lives."

Mabel and her uncle soon arrived at Aspendale Lodge, a lonely but comfortable dwelling, picturesquely situated on the slope of a wooded hill, with a large meadow spangled with daisies and buttercups behind it, from which the ascent was to take place.

Augustine helped Mabel to alight, and then leading her into his house, introduced her to Mr. Verdon, a small, lightly-built man, with sharp features, and an appearance of remarkable intelligence in his keen grey eyes. Mabel was so eager to see the balloon that she could not wait until she had partaken of the breakfast to which her drive and early rising had disposed her to do full justice, but hurried into the back field.

The huge ball was not yet inflated, but Mabel

looked with interest on the inert mass, which was so soon to rise as if instinct with life, and was full of eager questions, which the goodnatured æronaut, himself an enthusiast on the subject, took a pleasure in answering.

The breakfast was a very cheerful meal. Augustine had such a vast intellectual store always at his command, and Vernon was so completely master of the theme then most interesting to Mabel, that she listened, and occasionally joined in the conversation with the most keen delight. Then when the breakfast was concluded, and preparations were begun for inflating the balloon with gas, Mabel joyously flitted from meadow to hall, from hall to meadow, now watching Mr. Verdon's operations, now superintending those of the housekeeper, busy in laying out the elegant collation which Augustine had ordered for his guests. Mabel was in her element, in her glory! She was to do the honours of her uncle's house, receive her uncle's guests ; and this to a lively girl of fifteen was a dignity of no common order !

As carriage after carriage arrived, Mabel welcomed every new comer, imitating Ida's manner as well as her overflowing spirits would let her. It was her chief pleasure to tell every friend whom she knew, that she herself was to go in the balloon, to hear this one marvel at her courage, and that one envy her rare fortune,—to feel herself something of a heroine, an object of attention to those around her.

Dr. Bardon was one of the earliest arrivals at Aspendale Lodge. His first question was, "Has the earl come ?"

Mabel replied, " Not yet;" and he gave a malicious smile.

" What does the countess say to this?" inquired Mabel; " did she know that you were coming to the Lodge?"

" I can scarcely make out what she knows or does not know, what she likes or does not like," said the doctor gruffly ; " but I suspect she'll look out for the balloon. The wind, I see, is from the east ; 'twill bear you in the direction of Mill Cottage."

The circle of guests would now have been complete, but for the non-arrival of one. That one was most eagerly watched for. The oft-repeated question, " Has the earl come?" was now exchanged for another, "Will the earl come?" and jests were made, and bets were laid, while every minute that elapsed added to the impatience of the party.

A large concourse of people had gathered in a neighbouring field, drawn from a circuit of many miles to see the ascent of the *Eaglet.* Ayrton had sent its labourers, Pelton its shopboys and mechanics; the ploughman had left his team, and merry farmers' wives had forsaken their dairies, and come with their children and grandchildren to witness the wonderful sight. The hedge which surrounded Augustine's meadow was lined and double lined with the eager heads of such spectators as these, while around the balloon itself gathered a brilliant circle of gaily-dressed guests, privileged to occupy a nearer place.

The great striped ball had now been swelled to its utmost dimensions, and swayed gently to and fro, as if luxuriating in the sense of power, only restrained by a number of strong ropes from bursting upwards towards the skies.

" It is like swollen pride," observed Mabel, " impatient to mount aloft."

"And puffed out with the idea of its importance, like the fools of this world," added the doctor; "but," he continued with a sardonic sneer, "good strong cords of prudence will keep the most aspiring down !"

Augustine was annoyed at the sarcasm, and the pretty general remark now occasioned by the non-arrival of Dashleigh. Mr. Verdon had quite completed his preparations. In the gaily painted wicker car, ornamented with little fluttering flags, the ballast had been carefully placed, together with the grappling irons, a case of instruments to be used by Augustine for scientific purposes, and "last, not least," a basket containing some refreshments, and two bottles of sparkling champagne.

Mabel was becoming almost wild with impatience, when suddenly the heads of the outside spectators were turned round in an opposite direction from that of the balloon, and then hats and handkerchiefs waved in the air, and cheer after cheer from the rural crowd announced to the more select circle that the long-expected was coming at last. Presently a chariot, with servants in red liveries, and a coronet on the panel, dashed up the hill to Aspendale Lodge! Mabel could not refrain from clapping her hands. "He is come! he is come!" the murmur ran through the crowd, and the guests assembled in the meadow simultaneously directed their gaze towards the house. Augustine, with a sense of relief, hurried in to greet his illustrious guest at the front entrance. After the lapse of some minutes he emerged from the dwelling, and crossed his back garden on his way to the meadow; while at his side, pale and silent as a corpse, walked Reginald, Earl of Dashleigh.

CHAPTER XXI.

THE ASCENT.

"The brave man is not he who feels no fear
For that were stupid and unnatural ;
But he whose spirit triumphs o'er his fear,
And boldly dares the danger Nature shrinks from."

JOANNA BAILLIE.

HAS the reader ever pictured to himself what, at the time of the Reign of Terror, must have been the emotions of some noble victim borne towards the fatal guillotine ? Imagine the sensations of some nobleman, fostered in the lap of luxury, accustomed to every indulgence, full of the pride of birth, when the rolling death-cart brings him suddenly in view of the horrible engine of destruction, and the dense crowd of eager spectators assembled to witness his cruel end ! A sense of personal dignity struggles with that of mortal fear. He must not show the inward agony that chills his shuddering frame ; he must be firm and calm before the gaze of those thousand curious eyes ; and yet the horror of that hour almost overcomes his self-command, and he fears that his resolution may give way in the fiery trial !

He who can realize to himself this picture, will be

able to enter into the sensations of the unhappy
earl, when from his carriage window he first beheld
the huge globe, towering high above the surrounding
crowd, and heard the sound of the cheers which
greeted his own tardy appearance on the spot. The
vain hopes which he had clung to vanished in a
moment from his mind. Mr. Verdon had not disappointed his friend,—no accident had marred the
balloon in its transit to Augustine's house; no, there
it was ready, quivering as if with eager joy to welcome its victim! How Dashleigh would have blessed
any mischievous urchin who should, by fire or steel,
have clipped for ever the wings of the *Eaglet!*

Let it not be supposed, however, that the Earl of
Dashleigh was a coward. The testimony borne by
Augustine Aumerle had been simply just. As a
soldier the earl would have done his duty, and earned
an honourable name; he would not have blenched
on a field of battle, and if wounded, would have endured in silence the anguish caused by the probe or
the knife. But his physical constitution was such
that he could hardly look down from the height of
an ordinary wall without a giddy sensation. His
head seemed to turn round on the brink of a chasm,
and the horror of falling down a precipice haunted
him even in his dreams! It was not to be wondered
at that to such a man the idea of gazing down thousands of feet from the clouds was fraught with unutterable terror; and the earl looked so ill when

Augustine Aumerle came forth from the door to meet him, that his friend involuntarily exclaimed, " Dashleigh ! you are not fit to ascend ! "

"I must, I must," was the muttered reply, as with an ice-cold hand the earl returned the grasp of his host.

"Come first into the house and refresh yourself ; I am certain that you are not well ;" and so saying, Augustine led the way into a room where a cold collation had been spread out for his guests.

The earl walked up to the table, poured out a quantity of wine into a tumbler, and took it off at a draught. Augustine feared that there might be some risk that his friend would dull his intellect in the hope of strengthening his nerves.

The two then proceeded, as we have seen, through the garden into the meadow. The earl acknowledged the salutations of his acquaintance by stiffly bending his head, but never uttered a word.

" Will you go back?" whispered Augustine, who began to feel uneasy as to the result of the experiment before him.

The earl hesitated for an instant, only an instant; he caught sight of Dr. Bardon, watching him with a sarcastic smile on his face, which stung the proud noble like a scorpion; pushing forward with a determined effort, Reginald sprung into the car in which Mabel, with girlish impatience, had already taken her place.

" Now we only want Verdon," observed Augustine, more leisurely following his companion ; "he is busy giving last orders, but he will be with us in a minute."

"And then, skyward ho!" exclaimed Mabel, whose heart beat high with excitement and pleasure, which was only heightened by a slight touch of feminine fear.

Whether it were the effect of her words, or of the somewhat rocking motion given to the car, even while resting on the grass, by the swaying of the huge ball above it,—or whether the wine too hastily taken had risen into the brain of the earl, was a point never clearly decided; but at this moment the nervousness of Dashleigh suddenly rose to a pitch which entirely mastered his judgment. Rising from his seat with an agitated air, he attempted to push past Augustine, in order to get out of the car. His friend, extremely annoyed at the thought of so public an exhibition of weakness, laid his hand on the arm of the earl ; but this slight action seemed only to rouse the miserable man to frenzy.

" Let go!" exclaimed Dashleigh, in a voice so loud that it resounded to the utmost edges of the crowd; . " Let go!" echoed a thousand voices, believing it to be the signal for ascent !   The men who were grasping the ropes instantly obeyed the word, and almost with the sudden effect of an explosion, the immense balloon darted upwards to the sky, shrinking before

the upturned eyes of the breathless spectators, till
its vast globe gradually dwindled to the apparent
size of the plaything of a child!

There were deafening cheers from the crowd
beyond the hedge; "Bravo! bravo! off she goes!"
shouted stentorian voices; but on the faces of the
nearest spectators were painted fear and dismay, as
Mr. Verdon—interrupted in the midst of hurried
directions by the sudden cry and shout, stretched
out his hands wildly towards the receding balloon,
and exclaimed in a tone of anguish,—"Merciful
Heaven! they are lost!"

"Lost! what do you mean, man?" exclaimed
Bardon, coming forward in his blunt manner to give
a voice to the fears of the rest. "And how does it
happen that you are not in the car?"

"The signal was given too soon!" cried Verdon,
his nervous accents betraying his emotion. "I was
just questioning my assistant as to the working of
the valve, for I thought that something seemed
wrong with the rope, when a voice shouted out,
'Let go!' and the idiots took that for the signal."

"But you do not apprehend danger?" cried a
gentleman near.

"Danger!" repeated Verdon impatiently; "why,
Aumerle knows no more of the management of a
balloon than a child;—Heaven only knows if we
shall ever look on their faces again!"

Terror, wonder, compassion, now spread rapidly

through the assembled throng; lip after lip repeating
the tale with its own comments and exaggerations.
Exclamations of pity and grief resounded on all
sides, as straining eyes attempted to pierce the cloud
which soon hid the *Eaglet* from view.   Once it was
visible for a few minutes, and little dim specks
could be distinguished in the car, which were known
to be the living human beings who had so lately
been standing in health and strength on that very
spot !   It was a sickening reflection that they were
now utterly beyond reach of man's aid, drifting
away at the mercy of the winds, perhaps to some
terrible fate which might be guessed at, but never
known.   None, perhaps, felt the revulsion more
terribly than Timon Bardon.   He who had exulted
in revenge, found the cup which he had grasped
so eagerly, and deemed so sweet, suddenly changed
to a burning poison.   His fierce, strong nature made
his sense of suffering peculiarly acute.   " How shall
I tell this to Annabella?" was the distracting thought
uppermost in his mind, as throwing himself on a
horse which had been lent to him for the occasion,
he dashed wildly along the road which led to his
little home.

CHAPTER XXII.

IN THE CLOUDS.

"How fearful
And dizzy 'tis to cast one's eyes so low !
. . . . . I'll look no more
Lest my brain turn, and the deficient sight
Topple down headlong ! "   SHAKSPEARE.

"OH, how delightful !" was the first exclamation of
Mabel, as the *Eaglet* shot upwards, swiftly, but
with a motion so smooth that its speed was only
made known by the earth and the spectators appearing
to sink down—down—ever growing less and less,
while the cheers sounded fainter and fainter, as
rising up from a distance.   "How delightful!" she
repeated, waving a little flag as her farewell to those
below.

But when the smiling Mabel turned to look at
her companions, she was somewhat startled to mark
that the countenance of her uncle was of the same
ashen hue as that of the earl.

"How is it that Mr. Verdon is not with us?"
exclaimed Mabel in some surprise.

Augustine silenced her by a warning look.   His
grasp on the arm of Dashleigh had grown heavier
N

and tighter; but for that grasp it is possible that the
nobleman, in the first excitement of fear, would
have flung himself out of the car. Augustine's first
thought was for his companion, for he felt that the
unhappy Dashleigh was trembling convulsively under
his hand.

"Well, my friends," said he, in a tone so cheerful
that it completely deceived his niece; "Verdon will
think it a shame if we do not go back for him
directly; I propose, therefore, that we descend."

"Yes, descend!" cried Dashleigh wildly; and a
strange faint echo from the far earth repeated the
word, "Descend!"

Augustine was almost afraid to loosen his hold
on the arm of the earl; it was, however, necessary
that he should try some means of bringing the
Eaglet to the ground. He was, of course, aware
that this means must be to let out the gas which inflated the ball, but ignorant as he was of the practical
working of a balloon, however easily he might grasp
its theory, Augustine was left to guess the way in
which this effect might be produced. Mabel, who
had perfect confidence in the power of her gifted
uncle to master any difficulty, and who saw no
change in his countenance except the paleness which
overspread his handsome features, had no idea of the
anxious fear which now perplexed his mind.

Augustine laid hold of a rope which seemed to
him to be the one most probably attached to the

valve at the top of the ball, and in this his reason had not misled him. The valve was constructed to open inwardly, so that the pressure of the gas within might keep it constantly closed, except when mechanical means were applied to counteract that pressure. But Mr. Verdon's misgiving had not been without foundation; there was some hitch with the valve which prevented its working properly under an inexperienced hand. As Augustine pulled the rope, the balloon entered into a cloud, and the travellers suddenly found themselves enveloped in a dense, damp, chilly mist.

" Are we ascending or descending?" asked Mabel, " for the balloon is so steady that it does not seem to be moving at all."

Her uncle, who, with far greater anxiety, had been asking himself the same question, replied in a voice still perfectly calm, "throw down some pieces of paper, and we shall ascertain that fact directly."

Wondering that he should not know it without having recourse to experiment, Mabel immediately obeyed. " The bits seem to fall, not like paper, but like lead!" she exclaimed.

" Then we must be ascending rapidly still," muttered Augustine; and he pulled the rope with such desperate force that it snapped in his hand, and all communication with the all-important valve was broken off for ever!

" God have mercy upon us!" was Augustine's

instinctive prayer, not uttered aloud from the fear of
alarming his companions. The thick mist prevented
Mabel from having any clear idea of what her uncle
was doing, but she thought him strangely silent, and
a damping chill came over her young spirit like the
fog which enwrapped her form. Augustine looked
up almost in despair at the huge indistinct mass
looming as a dark cloud above him. Oh! that there
were but any means of tearing open a passage for the
gas! The wicker car, suspended by ropes, hung too
low beneath the ball for it to be possible for
Aumerle's extended arm to reach the silken globe,
or his penknife would have at once offered an easy
solution of the difficulty. A light, agile sea-boy
might possibly have climbed one of the ropes, and
so have reached the inflated ball; but the brain of
Augustine turned dizzy at the very thought of
attempting to clamber at the awful height to which
he knew that he must now have attained. His
frame was remarkable for strength as well as for
manly beauty, but was altogether unfitted for a
perilous feat like this. To have attempted it must
have been inevitably to fall and perish.

Suddenly, to Mabel's relief, the balloon emerged
from its misty shroud, and burst again into the
brightness of day. The scene was one never to be
forgotten, but Mabel was the only one of the travellers whose mind was sufficiently at ease to enjoy
its sublime and awful beauty.

Above was the sky—deeply, intensely blue, such
as in Italy meets the enchanted gaze. Below was a
floor of pure white cloud, spread out, as it appeared
to Mabel, like a vast sea of cotton, on which lay
piled here and there vast masses, or islands of snow.
Some of these masses were floating beneath them
with a slow and majestic motion, impelled by cur-
rents of wind which did not reach the strata of air
to which the balloon had ascended. Presently the
white floor seemed gradually to part on either side,
and an opening appeared through which a strange
panoramic view of the earth burst on the wondering
eye. It lay—Oh! how far beneath! There was no
distinction of mountain or plain, a dim blue hue
tinted all. In the words of a former aeronaut,—
" The whole appeared a perfect plain, the highest
building having no apparent height, but reduced all
to the same level, and the whole terrestrial prospect
seemed like a coloured map." There lay Dashleigh
Hall, the seat of ancestral pride, shrunk to the appearance of a tiny toy,—a mere nothing viewed
from that awful height, even as all earth's pomps
and grandeur must appear to those who survey them
from heaven. For the first time since he had worn
his honours, Dashleigh felt them no cause for pride.
He was in his own eyes no peer, no lofty aristocrat,
but a poor, weak child of man, with every nerve un-
strung, and an undefined horror hanging over him.
Gladly would he then have exchanged places with

the poorest peasant standing on solid ground, though not possessing a single foot of it.

"Look upwards—upwards—not downwards!" cried Augustine, alarmed at the wild expression on the haggard face of his friend. "Lie down, Dashleigh, at the bottom of the car, and fix your gaze on the sky above!"

"Uncle!" exclaimed Mabel, "how strange your voice sounds—like what one might hear in a dream; and my own, too, seems quite different from what it was when we were on the ground."

"This is the effect of the rarified air upon the ear."

"Uncle, the objects below us grow smaller and smaller, we must be rising higher and higher; I thought that you meant to descend."

Augustine's only reply was a look which in an instant, as by a lightning flash, revealed to the young girl the full danger of their situation.

"You cannot descend!" she gasped forth, clasping her hands in terror.

"Remember *him*," said Augustine in a very low voice; "if he knew our helpless condition, I believe that it would turn his brain."

"But cannot you tell how to let out the gas?"

"I cannot—"

"You who know everything—"

"I do not know this."

Mabel sank back upon the seat from which she

had half risen while addressing her uncle, who, holding firmly by a rope, was standing upright in the car. She was a brave girl, and acted as such; she neither uttered cry nor shed tear, but she turned very pale and cold, and shivered as if mantled in ice. It gave her now a sickening oppression to gaze below. Was she never, never to return to that earth which lay beneath her—never again to be pressed to her father's heart—never to meet the smile of her sister! Was she to float on in these dreary regions never before visited by man, buoyed up in a moving coffin, till—"

The awful, death-like stillness was suddenly broken by a sharp report, sounding to the startled ears of the travellers something like that of a pistol! It was but a cork in the refreshment basket going off from the diminished pressure of the atmosphere causing the wine in the bottle to expand, but the explosion of a cannon could hardly have produced a more startling effect than a noise so sudden and so unexpected. Dashleigh sprang like a maniac from the bottom of the car, in which he had been quietly lying, and made a frantic attempt to throw himself out of the car. Augustine had to struggle and wrestle to keep him down, as one engaged in a contest for life; and the *Eaglet*, at the same time, passing into a violent current of air, rocked and shook, and swung to such an extent, that Mabel had to grasp tight hold of the wicker-work to prevent

herself from being flung down into the clouds which
again had closed beneath them.

The whirlwind grew yet more tremendous, tossing
to and fro the enormous balloon as if it had been a
bubble on the current, actually turning it round and
round, and making the car describe a wide swinging
circuit below it.

It was a very awful moment—a moment in which
the heart almost ceases to beat, and the only utterance of the soul can be a cry to the God that made
it!   It seemed as in answer to that instinctive
prayer to the ear that is never closed, that the
whirlwind soon appeared to lessen its violence, the
motion of the balloon abated, the frightful swinging
of the car ceased, and Augustine uttered a faint
"thank God!" while Dashleigh sank senseless at
his feet!

CHAPTER XXIII.

REGRETS.

There is no wretchedness where guilt is not;
  Religion can relieve the sharpest woes,
All—save remorse, be softened or forgot!
  But where can she—the hopeless, find repose
Whose anguish from her own transgression flows!
  My pride—my folly—bade a husband die,
His life embittered, hastened on its close!
  Yes, weep, ye who can weep,—but I—but I—
My heart weeps tears of blood,—and yet my eyes are dry!

THE mind of Ida was not quite satisfied that it was right in her sister to ascend in the *Eaglet*, contrary to the direct and positive prohibition of her step-mother. Ida could not help suspecting that she herself had not proved altogether a safe guide for her younger sister; she feared that while discouraging the expedition on the plea of danger, she had not sufficiently done so on the score of duty. The more Ida reflected on the subject, the more conscience reproached her for rather nurturing than repressing the spirit of independence which proudly rose against the control of Mrs. Aumerle, both in Mabel's heart and her own.

Ida was not one to deaden conscience by refusing to listen to its voice, and she arose on the morning

of the 12th resolved to use her strongest persuasions
to induce Mabel to give up her project. She went
to the room of her sister, but found it already empty;
and then proceeded to the garden, but Mabel had
left it some minutes before.

Ida felt that it was too late for her to undo any
mischief which might have been done, and made no
mention at the breakfast table of Mabel's intention
to ascend, not wishing to be the first to draw upon
her sister the displeasure of Mrs. Aumerle.

"Perhaps," thought Ida, "reflection has had the
same effect upon Mabel that it has had upon myself;
she may have come to the like conclusion that it
would be wrong to go in the car. I earnestly hope
that it may be so, for I feel a strange uneasiness at
the thought of her venturing aloft. Yet there can
be no real danger, or my uncle would never have
wished to take Mabel with him, nor my dear father
have half consented to her going up in the balloon.
If she only come back in safety I shall feel a weight
taken off my heart, and I shall in future more earnestly try to lead her aright in all things."

About the hour of noon, as the vicar was writing
in his study, he was interrupted by the entrance of
Ida.

" Dearest Papa," said she, gently approaching him,
and seating herself at his feet, "forgive me for dis-
turbing you when you are busy, but I want your
permission to go and see Annabella again."

The vicar looked grave, but made no reply.

"When I last went to Mill Cottage with Mabel, and our cousin refused to see us, you said that it was your desire that we should leave her to herself for the present; but it is to-day, as you know, that her husband is to go up in the *Eaglet*, and I cannot help imagining how anxious and unhappy Annabella must be, because— "

"Because she has goaded him to the step," said the vicar.

"Somehow I am so restless to-day—I can neither read nor work,—and my heart draws me towards Annabella. I fancy—it may be presumption, but I fancy that her spirit may be softened just now, and that some word might be spoken which might make it more easy to reconcile her to her husband. Have I your consent to my going?"

"I will go with you, my child," said the vicar putting up his papers and locking his desk. "I believe that anything that we may say to that poor misguided girl will be likely to háve more effect during the absence of Dr. Bardon. Whatever may be the cause for his dislike, it is evident that he nourishes a strong prejudice against the Earl of Dashleigh."

It was not long before the father and daughter, bound on their errand of love, reached the cottage in which the countess had chósen to take up her abode. They were ushered into the sitting-room

where they found Cecilia bending pensively over a
piece of embroidery, and the countess with a book in
her hand, which she had, however, only taken up as
a device for silencing conversation, as during the last
half-hour she had not turned over a leaf.

Miss Bardon welcomed her guests with smiles;
Annabella with a stiff politeness, which said as distinctly as manner could convey meaning, "There must
be no entering upon any disagreeable subject of conversation; the parson must not preach, nor the friend
attempt to persuade."

Ida's heart yearned over her cousin, but she had
not courage to break through that formidable barrier
of reserve. The vicar saw that the first sentence
bordering upon reproof would be the signal for his
niece to quit the apartment. Disappointed, but not
yet disheartened, the good man inwardly prayed that
He who can alone order the unruly wills and affections of his sinful creatures, would bend the proud
spirit of the haughty girl, and open her eyes to her
error. Little did he dream of the manner in which
that prayer would be answered!

As might be imagined, under the circumstances the
conversation was constrained; Miss Bardon princi-
pally sustained it, for she was the only one present
who could talk at ease on all the trifling topics of
the day.

"Hark!" exclaimed Cecilia suddenly, "there is a
horse running away!" and her words seemed con-

firmed by so rapid a clatter of hoofs, that not only Ida, but Aumerle and the countess followed her quickly to the open door to see if some rider were not in peril.

The alarm was in one sense a false one ; the horse that came galloping on was impelled to furious speed by the whip and the spur of its rider, as if—

"Headlong haste or deadly fear
Urged the precipitate career ; "

and the party saw with surprise that this rider was Dr. Bardon. He reined up so suddenly at the garden-gate that the panting steed was thrown violently back on its haunches. The doctor flung himself quickly from the saddle, and without even pausing to throw the rein round a post, advanced to the party at the door. His long white hair streamed wildly back from his excited face.

" Something has happened !" exclaimed Ida ; Anna-bella's tongue seemed to cleave to the roof of her mouth !

" The balloon !" cried Cecilia ; " tell us, oh ! tell us, has some accident befallen the balloon ?"

The gesture of Bardon was one which might well have beseemed a prophet of desolation, as raising his arm he exclaimed, " Lost ! lost ! past recovery !"

" How lost ?—what would you have us believe ?—remember in whose presence you speak !" cried Law-rence Aumerle almost sternly.

" I cannot mince my tale," was the gloomy reply,

"nor deal out poison by drops. By some fatal mistake the balloon was let off before the car had been
entered by the only man who could guide it. We
are never likely to hear anything more of it, or the
unfortunate beings within it!"

"Who were in it?" exclaimed the Aumerles in one
breath. "Who were in it?" echoed the countess in a
sepulchral voice, fixing upon Bardon an eye which
sought to read in his face a sentence of life or death.

"Augustine Aumerle was there—and Mabel—"

The father uttered an exclamation of anguish, and
Ida staggered backwards, closing her eyes, as if a
poniard had stuck her.

"And—and—the Earl of Dashleigh!"

Annabella gave such a piercing cry as agony might
wring from a wretch upon the rack, and would have
sunk on the earth but for the support of her uncle.

"There may be hope yet,—God is merciful,—He
will have compassion on us,—let us pray, let us pray!"
exclaimed the vicar, in the sight of the misery of
another seeming half to forget his own.

"See—see!" exclaimed Cecilia, suddenly pointing
towards the sky.

There was breathless silence in a moment, and
every eye was eagerly turned in the same direction.
A small dark object appeared aloft, floating far, far
higher than wing of bird ever could soar! Who
can describe the intensity of the agonizing gaze fixed
by father—sister—wife, upon that little distant ball?

Arms were wildly stretched towards it, but not a word was uttered, scarce a breath was drawn while it yet remained in sight. Even when it had disappeared, the upwards-gazing group seemed almost as if transfixed into stone; till Bardon, with rough kindness, attempted to draw Annabella back into the cottage, muttering, "I feel for you, from my soul I do!"

"Feel for me!" exclaimed the countess, shrinking from his touch with an expression of horror, her pent-up anguish finding vent in passionate upbraiding; "you who led me to this abyss of misery, you who roused up my accursed pride, you who made me write words which I would now only too gladly blot out with my heart's blood! But for you I might have listened to truth; but for you I might never have left the true friends to whom I turn in my agony now! Oh, may God forgive you," she added wildly,—"God help me to forgive you, but never, never enter my presence—never let me behold you again!"

And so they parted, the tempter and the tempted— the countess to return to the vicarage with her almost heart-broken companions, Dr. Bardon to brood in his solitary cottage over deep, unavailing regrets!

In the dark abode of endless woe thus may bitter recrimination deepen the anguish of the lost, when some wretched soul recognises the author of his misery in one called on earth his friend, who had stirred up his evil passions, and pampered his fatal pride!

CHAPTER XXIV.

SOARING ABOVE PRIDE.

> " By grace divine my heart towards Thee draw,
> By due afflictions check presumptuous pride,
> With hope and love turn fell despair aside,
> And make my chief delight Thy holy law ! "
>   ROBERT TUDOR TUCKER.

THE great red sun, like a huge globe of fire, was sinking in the west,—I would have said the horizon, but
that word gives the idea of a point nearly level with
the eye, while the orb appeared far beneath them to
the travellers in the *Eaglet.*   The red light tinted
with a fiery glow the lower hemisphere of the balloon,
which was all that met the eye of the earl, for he
had cautiously abstained for many hours from glancing downwards towards the earth.

Dashleigh was now perfectly calm, though silent
and thoughtful.   That one fearful day had effected
upon the young nobleman the work of years. Deeply
solemn were his reflections.   With a conscience
neither dead nor unenlightened, the earl had needed
no prophet to decipher for him the fiery " letters on
the wall " of affliction.   Heavily and yet more heavily
had descended on him the Almighty's chastening

hand, and every blow had evidently been aimed at his pride! Had he not been humiliated in the presence of his friend,—satirized by his wife, ridiculed by the world, and had he not now by an unconquerable weakness, which a girl would have blushed to betray, been the actual cause of the fearful position in which he and his companions appeared! Bitter, bitter was the humiliation of the proud man! Had he been destitute of the faith which supports, and the hope which cheers, Dashleigh would have been utterly crushed by the successive strokes laid upon him. But in him there was much of the gold, which beneath the hammer "does not break, but extend." Dashleigh resembled less the son of Kish whom trial drove into fierce despair, than the haughty Assyrian king who, having endured that most humbling degradation which was the appointed punishment for pride, "lifted up" his "eyes unto heaven," and "blessed the most High," with a spirit subdued.

Strangely had passed the day; as light as the feather down, the balloon floated in the ocean of air. The party in the car had partaken of the slight refreshment which had been provided, in little expectation that even that would be required during a two hours' expedition. Beverage there was none, for the wine had exploded both the bottles from the cause mentioned in a preceding chapter. The lips of each of the sufferers was parched and dry, and a painful sensation of thirst was added to the trials of the hour.

o

Augustine and Mabel had exhausted all their inventive powers in contriving means to cut an opening in the ball of the balloon. Several attempts had been made, but all had ended in disappointment. The knife, flung upwards with a steady hand, had glanced back from the varnished silk, and fallen through depths which the mind shuddered to calculate. Every effort but strengthened the conviction that all effort was unavailing.

There had been silence for a long time in the car,—silence of which dwellers upon earth can scarcely form a conception. There was here no rustling leaf, no buzz of an insect's wing to break the awful stillness! Motion itself was impalpable, being unaccompanied by the slightest sound!

"Augustine," said the earl, raising himself on his elbow, for he still in a reclining posture occupied the lower part of the car, "do you believe that you can hide from me the fact that you have no power over the balloon; that our condition is hopeless?"

"Nay," replied his friend, "let us never despair. The gas may yet find some vent. There was never yet balloon made so air-tight that it would not leak in the course of time."

Mabel thought that she had never seen the pale delicate features of the earl invested with such true dignity, as when with low, but distinct utterance he made his reply: "I would rather look the danger in the face. My brain is not dizzy now,—none are dizzy who look above rather than below them. I have a presentiment that we shall never reach the ground alive."

Not a word was uttered in contradiction or reply, and the earl continued in the same calm, deliberate tone: "Death is a great preacher, Augustine; he tells us startling truths! He tarnishes with a touch the gilding on objects that once appeared to us bright! He levels the prince and the peasant. He has been preaching to me a soul-searching sermon, and from a very solemn text."

"What is the text?" inquired Augustine, while Mabel bent forward to listen.

"*The loftiness of man shall be bowed down and the haughtiness of man shall be laid low, and the Lord alone shall be exalted in that day.*"

Again there was solemn, deathlike silence! Perhaps, as Mabel and her uncle sat watching the last edge of the sun's disc disappear, and the sky gradually darken into night, the self-reliant genius, the high-spirited girl, were secretly applying to themselves the sublime words of the prophet of Judah.

While twilight still lingered, a thought struck Mabel. She remembered that she had brought with her an envelope ready directed to her sister, with a sheet of blank paper enclosed, for her fancy had been pleased with the idea of dating a letter from "the clouds." Making a table of her seat in the car, Mabel knelt down, and with a pencil wrote a sad

and touching farewell to the parent and sister so
tenderly loved. Many names were kindly remembered
in that note, for the proud spirit of Mabel was
softened and subdued by the pressure of trial, and
no one was then recalled to her mind but with a
feeling of kindness.   To her step-mother Mabel sent
a long message.   She confessed her fault with frank
regret, and asked the pardon of Mrs. Aumerle, not
only for the last act of open disobedience which was
now so fearfully punished, but for a long course of
petty provocations, for sullen looks, and proud retorts,
and bitter words spoken against her; Mabel entreated
forgiveness for all.   Her tears dropped fast upon
the sheet—the first tears which she had shed on
that day, but she dashed them hastily from her eyes.
Mabel then folded the note and kissed it, as if
believing that the paper might bear to her home
the impress of that last token of love ; then she
dropped her letter over the side of the car, watching
it as it descended, and picturing to herself the grief
and tenderness with which it would be received, and
read, and treasured up as a mournful memorial of
her of whose fate it might be the only record.

Dashleigh had watched the action of his young
companion, and now drew from his vest a small but
very elegant pocket-book, which bore on one side an
embossed gold shield, on which his name was en-
graved, surmounted by his coronet.   This was the
first gift of affection which the young nobleman had

received from his affianced bride. It had been his constant companion since the hour when he had received it from her hand. Dashleigh opened the book, and gazed for some moments on the inscription written on the fly-leaf, though the thickening darkness would have rendered it difficult to decipher, had he not known every syllable by heart. The earl then, rather by feeling than sight, traced two words on one of the blank pages, reclasped the book, and gave it to Mabel with an expressive movement of the hand. Sadly and silently she dropped into the dark abyss the love token of the unhappy Annabella.

More than an hour elapsed before the silence again was broken. The thin air of these upper regions had become intensely cold, and Mabel shivered in her spring attire. The balloon was drifting steadily on before the night breeze, as was marked by its dark globe appearing to blot out one constellation after another from the sky as it swept on, the sole object that broke the immense expanse of the star-lit heavens.

" I think," observed Mabel with a heavy sigh, "that all in my father's house must now be met together for evening prayers." She paused, as fancy brought before her eye the warm lighted room, the curtains drawn, the lamp-light falling on so many dear familiar faces ! Mabel thought how her father's voice would tremble as he uttered his fervent supplications for those in such awful peril, and how Ida would try to smother her bursting sobs, that she might not unnerve him by the sound of her distress. "They will be praying for us," continued Mabel; "should we not pray together—even here?"

"None have more need of prayer," murmured the earl; Augustine's head was bowed in assent.

"God is with us—even in this awful, awful height where no human being can approach us," faltered Mabel.

"Augustine Aumerle," said Lord Dashleigh, "do you lead our evening devotion."

"Any one rather than me!" exclaimed Augustine; "none so unfit—so unworthy—so incapable!"

And there was truth in these strange words. To the gifted scholar, the eloquent orator, the language of prayer was not familiar, the spirit of prayer had long, alas! been unknown! Augustine had indeed, during his visit to his brother, usually joined in the family devotions, but he had done so from courtesy to man, not from reverence for God. Unconvinced of the weakness or sinfulness of his own nature, he had sought neither pardon nor aid; he had felt no need of a divine sustaining power, for he had contentedly rested on his own. Augustine had made an idol of Intellect, with Pride for its priest, under the much abused name of Reason. What marvel that with all his knowledge Augustine knew not how to pray!

The earl felt the difficulty almost as strongly as his friend, though from a different cause. He had never been disturbed by a doubt on the subject of religion, and had from his earliest youth regarded revealed truth with reverence, and acts of worship with respect; but he had carried even into his devotion the cold formality which naturally followed an overweening sense of personal dignity. Dashleigh had been a regular attendant at church; but with the shy reserve of his nature, it would have seemed to him, till that night, impossible to have poured forth in the hearing of man an extempore prayer to his God. But where Pride is humbled, the spirit of supplication may rest. Never had the peer so felt before the littleness of personal distinctions; never, therefore, before had his heart been so attuned to simple prayer. As Augustine shrank from leading the devotions, which each one present felt would be at once the source of comfort and the fulfilment of duty, the nobleman, with folded hands, repeated aloud the first petitions in the Litany which instinct rather than memory suggested to his mind. Augustine and his young niece in low and earnest tones echoed the cry for mercy upon miserable sinners; and when it was followed by the comprehensive prayer, " in all time of our tribulation, in all time of our wealth, in the hour of death, and in the day of judgment—*Lord, deliver us!*" arose in solemn unison from three voices and three hearts. Never had the supplication been more earnestly, more fervently breathed.

The Lord's Prayer concluded the brief service, which for the time made that little car appear as a floating temple. The chill cloudy solitude seemed less terrible when the name of the Giver of all good, the Fount of all blessings, had sounded within it. Those who had prayed together, felt their souls more knit together, and more prepared to meet with firmness whatever the dark, drear night might bring. Philosophy had brought no comfort, earthly rank no relief, but the sense of the presence of a heavenly Father was as balm to the suffering sinking soul.

CHAPTER XXV.

A BROKEN CHAIN.

In the world's battle-field,
  Though the strife may be glorioι s,
The Tempter may yield,
  And our Faith be victorious;
In the deep soul alone
  Can the *last* stroke be given,
To God only known
  And the angels of heaven.

THE grief of Annabella and of Ida partook of the nature of their several characters; one was violent and passionate, the other quiet and deep. In the strong revulsion of feeling and anguish of remorse, the countess could scarcely remember a fault in him whom she had lately stigmatised as tyrannical, and satirized as weak. The earl's tragical fate seemed to throw a halo around him, and his wife remembered him but as the tender wooer, the affectionate husband, the dignified, yet courteous nobleman, graceful in person, lofty in principle—who had sought and won the heart of a girl whose pride, petulance, and passion, had destroyed the man whom she loved ! Annabella tore her beautiful hair, and struck her bosom, as if she would have wreaked vengeance

on herself for the fearful ruin that her folly had
wrought !

Ida found that her presence could afford no consolation to her cousin ; and then, not till then, she
hastened up to Mabel's little room, now again to
become her own, and falling on her knees by the
bedside, buried her face in her hands, and poured
forth an agonized prayer.   She remained long in the
same position, and then arose trembling and pale.
Every object in the room seemed to awaken a fresh
burst of sorrow.   There was Ida's own likeness on
the wall, sketched by the hand of Mabel,—a rough,
unfinished drawing, indeed, but yet a labour of love.
There were fragrant lilac blossoms from the favourite
bush which Mabel always called her "Ida," and
there on the toilette table lay a small Bible, Mabel's
birthday gift from her sister, where many a mark
and double mark showed that it had at least been
perused with interest and attention.   This Bible
now afforded the most soothing consolation to the
aching heart of Ida.

Mrs. Aumerle had been far more astonished than
pleased at the unexpected return of the countess,
until she learned its sad cause.   Her feelings then
became of a very mingled nature.   The danger of
the party in the balloon, and the grief of those left
behind, excited her heartfelt pity ; but her soul
vibrated between that emotion, and indignation at
the conduct which had occasioned the tragic event.

When the lady thought of the countess's pride, or the wilful disobedience of Mabel, she could not shut out from her mind the reflection that they had brought all their trouble upon themselves. Mrs. Aumerle's predominating sensation, however, was sympathy with her afflicted husband, and she did everything that lay in her power to inspire him with the cheering hopes that were strong within her own bosom.

"Nay, Lawrence, give not way to despair; this agrees neither with reason nor religion. Depend upon it everything will turn out far better than you could expect. The balloon will come down quietly to earth as other balloons have done, and we shall have the whole party sitting here—perhaps to-morrow, talking over their adventures, and smiling at our alarm. Don't tell me that your brother knows nothing about guiding a balloon—he is so wonderfully clever that he knows everything by intuition. He will find some method of getting safely out of the difficulty; my mind always grows easier when I think what a genius he is!"

Aumerle was walking up and down in his study, as if motion could relieve his mental distress, at each turn pausing at the window to look anxiously out upon the sky. He stopped short as his wife concluded her last sentence, and murmured, "My poor, poor brother! the bitterest trial of all is the fear that he is unprepared for the awful change!"

"This very trial may be sent to prepare him for it, to make him think more than he has ever yet done of the one thing that is needful. And our poor wilful Mabel—"

"Oh! blame not her—blame not her!" exclaimed Ida, who had entered as Mrs. Aumerle was speaking, and who now bent at her stepmother's feet in a posture of humiliation as well as of grief; "you and my dear father must learn how much of her fault rests with me. It is a bitter confession, but I can find no peace till it is made. Dear Mabel came to me yesterday evening, and told me that Papa had given a kind of permission to her to ascend in the *Eaglet*, bidding her at the same time consult you—"

' I positively forbade her," interrupted the lady.

"I know it—she told me all—and had I done my duty," continued Ida, her voice hardly articulate through sobs, "I would have told her that your refusal was sufficient—that she should submit and obey. But somehow—I can scarcely recall in what way—a chord of pride was touched in my own sinful heart; I felt it difficult to urge on her a duty which I had so often neglected myself, and I can now scarcely hope for my father's forgiveness, or yours, or my own—"

The last words were sobbed forth on the bosom of Mrs. Aumerle, for Ida's lowly confession had made her step-mother forget everything but the sister's grief and repentance, and no parent could more kindly have strained to her heart a beloved and penitent child, than the hard, severe, practical Barbara Aumerle embraced the daughter of her husband. Her tones were those of maternal tenderness and sympathy for the sorrower as she said, " Don't reproach yourself, darling,—don't reproach yourself, I believe there were faults on both sides!"

The vicar, with moist eyes and a thankful heart, saw for the first time cordial sympathy between two beings whom he dearly loved ; and Pride fled in gloomy disappointment from the scene, for he knew that the chain of his captive was broken !

CHAPTER XXVI.

THE AWFUL CRISIS.

"Oh! how sweet to feel and know
E'en in this hour of dread, that dear to Thee
Is the confiding spirit!"

           E. TAYLOR.

"Henceforth I learn that to obey is best,
And love with fear the only God; to walk
As in His presence; ever to observe
His providence, and on Him sole depend,
Merciful over all His works, with good
Still overcoming evil, and by small
Accomplishing great things, by things deemed weak
Subverting wordly strong, and worldly wise
By simply meek!"

           MILTON.

IT is the darkest hour of night, that hour which precedes the dawn. A thousand stars are spangling the deep azure of the sky, looking down, like angels' eyes, on a world of sin and sorrow. Augustine's gaze is fixed upon one beauteous planet, which, in its calm light, outshines the tremulous glory of the constellations. Mabel has wearily fallen asleep where she sits, resting her head on her arm, the piercing cold of the upper air making her slumber the deeper. The earl, still stretched at the bottom of the car, is also finding a short oblivion of woe, and in dreams is wandering again upon the warm, bright, joyous earth, with Annabella at his side.

Augustine, on his dizzy height, in the stillness of the hour, feels himself alone with his God. The conversation held at the vicarage with his brother now recurs to his mind with a deep and solemn effect. Augustine draws a mental parallel between his own present awful position and that in which his soul has for so long unfearingly remained. Has he not been, as it were, floating between earth and heaven, carried up by his pride, full inflated as that swollen ball which is at this moment bearing him onward perhaps to destruction! Has he any reason to rejoice that he has risen high above the mass of his fellow-creatures, if his very exaltation prove the means of his deeper fall!

"Yes, fool that I was! I believed my intellect formed to pierce through the mists, to rise above the clouds, to find for itself a path that no mortal had discovered before! With proud presumption I refused the guidance of Faith in those regions to which Faith alone has access. I trusted to reason —philosophy—genius!—what have they done for me here? I have proved unequal even to the task of regulating the motions of this silken machine, yet I feared not to steer my own way through the vast mysteries of spiritual knowledge! As regards the soul as well as its mortal tenement, I have been the sport of the changing winds, enwrapt in the seething mist, struggling on through thickening darkness— and to what point now have I reached? I see the

calm, still stars above me, shining like the eternal
truths which audacious Pride once dared to question;
I view the orbs which for ages unnumbered have
kept their steady course through infinite space,
upheld by the Power and Wisdom whose mysteries
I vainly sought to fathom; earth's lights have all
faded and gone, the brightest illumine no more, the
clearest throw no ray on this darkness,—the gems
of the firmament alone, unchanged and unapproach-
able by man, are glittering over me still!

"Yes, I feel myself an atom in the vast universe
which is filled by God! And yet man's moral
responsibility—the awful trust of an immortal, an
accountable soul—give a fearful dignity to him still!
Am I fit to appear in the presence of Him before
whose throne I so soon may stand? Is there anything in myself to which I can cling for support in
the day of judgment? Can I plead my merits—my
virtues—my works? No; the truth is forced upon
me here, which mortal presumption so long refused
to acknowledge. As well might I fling myself from
this car, and falling a thousand fathoms hope to
reach the earth uninjured, as trust to find safety for
a guilty and sentenced soul without the one sacrifice
for sin, the atonement provided for those who with
child-like faith rest upon it, and it only!"

As Augustine pursued his solemn meditations,
gradually the stars became dimmer at the approach
of the dawn, even as the heavenly lights vouchsafed

to guide us here, will pale in the radiance of a more
perfect knowledge of a more glorious day; the deep
blue sky assumed a somewhat lighter hue, and the
looming outline of the balloon was seen more distinctly against it.

"Do my eyes deceive me," thought Augustine,
"or is the curve of that outline less bold than it
appeared in the light of the setting sun? It may
be but fancy, but it seems as though the ball were
less fully inflated; I could imagine that I even perceive what resembles a wrinkle in the silk. God in
mercy grant that this new hope be not an illusion!"
As he spoke, something like the smoke-wreath from
the mouth of a discharged cannon floated upwards
not far from the car, then another and another, all
ascending lightly from beneath, and mounting high
above the balloon.

"The clouds appear to rise!" exclaimed Augustine
eagerly; "a sure sign that we ourselves are descending!" He started from his seat, and grasping a
rope, looked over into the abyss.

The dim grey twilight scarcely yet sufficed to show
objects distinctly, though not a single cloud now
obscured the wide spreading prospect below. Augustine strained his eyes with gazing for several
minutes before he became fully assured of the nature
of what lay beneath him. One long faint streak of
red at length clearly defined the line where the sky
met the rounded horizon; there was no object, not

P

the smallest, to break that hard sharp line which
separated misty blue from deepening crimson; nor
swelling hill, nor rising mountain was there; Augustine's pulse beat quicker and he gasped as for breath,
for he was now convinced of two facts, each of
thrilling importance,—that the *Eaglet* was quickly
descending, and that it was descending into the
sea!

"The breeze must have borne us above the
Channel, and may bear us across it, if for but one
or two hours we can keep the balloon aloft! But
the gas is evidently fast escaping, and unless I
lighten the car, we shall soon be precipitated into
the wide waste of waters beneath!"

With almost the rapidity of thought, Augustine
caught up the large bag of ballast and flung it out
of the car. In the lapse of—as it seemed—two or
three minutes, a splashing sound distinctly came from
below, the first noise exterior to the car which had
reached the ear of Augustine for many a weary
hour. Slight as it was, it seemed sufficient to startle
the earl from his sleep; he opened his eyes, and gave
a little start of horror at the sight of the vast
ball above him, which in an instant brought back
to him the consciousness of what had occurred.

"Still this living death!" he exclaimed, and his
voice awakened Mabel.

"It is very, very cold," she murmured drowsily;
" and is the night really gone, and the beautiful

morning breaking? These soft rosy clouds are above us now, perhaps we may see—'

" Do not look down, Mabel !" cried her uncle.

But the word came too late,—the trembling girl was already surveying the broad, smooth ocean plain.

" Where can we be going ?" she exclaimed; " it is one flat blue expanse below, and there is a scent as if from the sea !"

" We must be over the Channel," said Dashleigh ; " Augustine Aumerle, what are you doing ?"

His friend had lifted up his box of instruments and flung it over the side ; the basket then followed. Augustine laid his hand on the grappling irons, but paused, till, at a shorter interval than before, the splash was heard from the sea.

" Are we sinking down ?" exclaimed Mabel and Dashleigh as if with one breath.

Augustine nodded an assent, and threw over the grappling irons. Nothing remained in the car which could be flung away to lighten the balloon.

" Oh ! what will become of us?—what will become of us ?" exclaimed Mabel, clasping her hands in terror, as death in a new form stared her in the face.

" Nothing will keep the balloon up," said Augustine Aumerle ; " we must commend our souls to a merciful God."

"Can you see no ship?" cried the earl; "no
object moving on the waters?" and starting up
in the eagerness of hope, he himself looked over
the side of the car, but almost sickening at the
dizzy prospect, sank back again to his place.

How gloriously burst the bright rays streaming
from the eastern horizon! how splendidly rose the
sun as a monarch rejoicing in his might, crimsoning
the floating clouds, and casting across the waters a
path of quivering gold! It struck the trembling
Mabel with a sense of awful beauty, as nearer and
nearer the *Eaglet* dropped toward ocean's liquid
grave! Again the coloured stripes of the ball shone
bright in the light of day, but it was with something
of horror that the travellers now regarded that which
Mabel had once playfully spoken of as an emblem of
swollen pride. It had carried them aloft through
the clouds to dreary, deathlike isolation, but failed
to support them now in the hour of peril and distress.

Down—down—down—yet with more rapid and
breathless descent, not in perpendicular fall, but
borne sideways by the freshening sea breeze, sank
the once towering *Eaglet*. The white crests of the
billows could now be distinguished, and even the fin
of a porpoise that flashed in the sunbeam.

"Might not the car float?" exclaimed Mabel; "it
is so buoyant and light!"

"It possibly might for a time," replied Augustine,

" were it not attached to this frightful incumbrance. Dashleigh," he asked suddenly, " have you a knife? I parted yesterday with mine."

" For what use ?" inquired the earl, as he gave a large one which he happened to have on his person.

There is no time for reply, the *Eaglet* is nearing the sea ; down—down—down—till with a violent shock which splashes the spray many feet into the air, the car strikes the waves and rebounds again, its dripping, gasping occupants clinging hard to prevent themselves from being flung out into the sea.

Down again—still with terrific violence; it is a frightful scene ! The spirit of a demon appears to animate the balloon,—a spirit that delights in torturing its miserable victims, as it goes sweeping, dashing, whirling on, now skimming at some height above the surface of the waters, now suddenly dipping so low that the half uttered shriek of Mabel is stifled in the gasping sob of suffocation ! No wretch fastened to a wild horse plunging, rearing, bounding on its way, with steaming nostril and foaming breath, ever endured the horrors of those dragged onward by that terrific engine of death, while the half submerged car leaves a long white bubbling track on the ocean !

Augustine alone loses not his presence of mind in this crisis of unutterable horror. Though the violent,

plunging, unsteady motion of the partly exhausted
balloon makes it difficult for his half drowned companions to keep their seats, he manages to retain his
footing without clinging, for both his hands are
engaged in a desperate effort to cut asunder the
cords of the balloon. It is their only chance of
life,—a miserable chance indeed, but better even to
sink at once in the watery depths, than to be thus
given again and again a horrible taste of death, to
be snatched away from it for a moment, only to be
precipitated downwards once more! With the
energy of despair the drowning man wields the
flashing knife, one after another the ropes are cut,
each that gives way rendering more fearful the
danger of the party—for at length the horizontal
position of the car is actually reversed, the wicker
is suspended by a single cord, and it is only by
clasping and clinging with strained muscles and
desperate grasp, that the terrified ones can retain
hold of this, the one frail barrier between themselves
and destruction !

Augustine awaits the moment when the lower end
of the car just touches the waves, and then the last
cord is severed! In an instant the light frame is
dashed on the billows, the waves splashing around
and over it and the three who almost miraculously
have retained their places within it. The car of
wicker work lined with oil-skin is not ill calculated
on an emergency to act the part of a boat, but it is

nearly full of water, and it is only by almost superhuman efforts in baling out the brine with Mabel's
straw hat and Dashleigh's beaver (Augustine's is
floating far on the waves) that the little shell can be
kept afloat.

In the meantime the balloon, released from the
weight of the car, bursts upwards like a bird of
prey soaring from a field of blood; or, to repeat
my former figure, as if the demon of pride, baffled
and wounded like Apollyon in his conflict with
Christian, had "spread his dark wings on the blast,
and fled away to his own habitation!" A wild
sensation of joy, even in the midst of her terror,
flashed across the mind of Mabel, as she saw that
terrible minister of destruction borne far away—and
for ever!

Perilous as was the situation of the voyagers in
their fragile boat, drenched as they were with salt
water, hungry, exhausted, their throats and lips
parched with burning thirst, they seemed but to
have exchanged one form of misery for another.
And yet the change from their late frightful position
brought with it some sense of relief. They were
touching, though not solid earth, yet some portion of
their native sphere; they were no longer floating in
an ocean of air, cut off by an impassable gulf from
the faintest hope of human assistance. There was
comfort in the sight of the lank brown sea-weed
borne on the floating waves, comfort in the sight of

the white winged birds that dipped in the flashing brine !

But as the day advanced endurance was sorely tried. Without rudder to steer the little car, or oar to propel, the sufferers could not shut out the prospect before them of almost certain death. The perpetual baling out of the water which leaked into their crazy boat, became an exhausting effort which their fainting frames could not for many hours sustain. Even Augustine's features began to acquire the rigid sternness of despair; and the earl, in silent supplication, commended a young widow to God.

Suddenly Mabel exclaimed with wild transport : " A sail, a sail in the horizon ! "

"But a sea-gull floating on the waves," replied Augustine, shading his eyes with his hand from the glare of a meridian sun.

The earl stretched out his blue corpse-like fingers in the direction indicated by Mabel, and then, raising his hand on high, exclaimed, " It is a sail— help is near—God be praised ! God be praised !"

Then followed a time of intense, almost madden-ing excitement. Augustine stood erect in the car, his tall form raised to its utmost height, as he waved again and again a kerchief as a signal of distress.

"Oh, if they should not see it !" exclaimed Mabel.

"Or seeing, disregard it," murmured the earl.

Again and again a shrill cry for help sounded

over the blue expanse. If the freshening breeze bore back that cry, so that it reached not the ears for which it was intended, that same breeze was filling the canvas and bringing near and more near the wished for,—the prayed for relief!

"I think that they see us!" cried Augustine, for the first time during that terrible day a gleam of joy. relaxing his features.

"Oh, my beloved father—my own Ida—shall I behold you again!" exclaimed Mabel.

"We must not relax our efforts," said her uncle, "or we shall perish even in the view of safety."

She speeds on,—the gallant bark,—dashing onwards "like a thing of life;" the figure of the steersman is now distinctly visible at her prow, his rough hail rings clear over the water,—was ever sight so welcome, was ever sound so sweet! Joy in that never-to-be-forgotten moment proves more overpowering even than terror, and the firmness which had stood the strain of most intense anxiety and fear gives way in the rebound of rapturous thanksgiving and delight!

CHAPTER XXVII.

TIDINGS.

"But rise, let us no more contend, nor blame
Each other, blamed enough elsewhere, but strive
In offices of love, how we may lighten
Each other's burden, in our share of woe."
                                        MILTON.

ON the eventful night which had been passed by the earl and his companions above the clouds, the mourners in the vicarage had known but little of repose. If oblivion came, it was in brief troubled snatches of slumber, from which the fevered sleeper awakes with a start to feel an icy oppression on the mind,—slumber which has in it nothing of refreshment.

All arose very early, with a vague yearning hope that tidings might come with the morning light, and the eager greeting when two of that anxious household met together was always, "Have you heard?—are there any tidings?"

Annabella would not appear at the breakfast table. Ida, pale as sculptured marble, scarcely able to swallow the nourishment of which she partook as a duty, sat beside her father, every sense absorbed in anxious listening. She heard the postman's step before she could see his form, and eagerly sprang forward to meet him, for it was possible—just possible—that he might be the bearer of news!

The man shook his head sadly when questioned; he had brought nothing but a parcel for the Countess of Dashleigh with the London post-mark upon it; and, with a sickening sense of disappointment, Ida bore it to the room of her cousin.

A strange gleam of hope flashed in the countess's large hollow eyes, as, without noticing the post-mark, she tore open the little packet; it was followed by a strange revulsion of feeling. There lay before her, beautiful in its fanciful binding of violet and gold, its glittering edges bright from the hand of the gilder, "THE FAIRY LAKE, *by the* COUNTESS OF DASHLEIGH."

There was a time when the youthful authoress would have gazed on the volume with delight, and turned over its pages with eager curiosity and pleasure! But now—there seemed written upon each a tale of wilful rebellion and insolent pride! Annabella flung her first book from her with an exclamation of anguish, for was it not connected in her mind with the fearful fate of her husband!

Then, with a sudden resolution, she rose from her seat, and hastily opened that desk at which she had penned her fatal article for the —— Magazine. Annabella would make some reparation, such reparation as yet was possible, for the deed so deeply

repented of. The countess wrote, with a hand that
shook so that she could scarcely form the letters, a
note to her publisher in London, bidding him at once
cancel the whole edition of her romance, prohibiting
him from selling a single copy of the work which he
had been hurrying through the press, and making
herself responsible for his losses, whatever they might
be. No earthly consideration would have induced
the miserable wife to delay, even for an hour, the
act by which she crushed the bud of hope, so long
eagerly fostered, at the very moment when it burst
into blossom ! The young authoress, once soaring so
high in the pride of literary ambition, was cutting
the cords of her balloon !

Almost every family in the neighbourhood, whether
rich or poor, called at the vicarage that day, impelled by friendship, curiosity, or pity, to inquire if
any tidings of the lost balloon had reached the
family of the Aumerles. No visitors, however, were
admitted, as soon as it was ascertained that they had
come to receive information, and not to give it.
The sound of wheels, and of frequent rings at the
gate, almost drove Annabella to distraction ! Ida
and her father spent much of the time together in
fervent prayer, but the miserable Countess of Dashleigh seemed too restless—too wretched to pray !

It was now the afternoon of one of the loveliest
days in the loveliest of seasons. The soft tinkling
of the distant sheep-bell, the low of the cattle in the

meadow, and the monotonous hum of the bee, came softly blended together to the ear. The bright mantle of sunshine fell on fruit-trees laden with blossom,—the hawthorn white with May's perfumed snow, the fragrant lilac, the laburnum dropping its showers of gold! Annabella gazed from the open casement of her apartment upon a lovely and varied prospect, but she had not the slightest perception of what lay directly before her eye.

Another loud ring! The countess turned her head with quick impatience. A man was standing at the gate. Was there something in his manner that announced the eager bearer of tidings, or did the wife intuitively grasp the fact that he brought her news of her husband? Ida seemed to have had the same perception, for, with the breeze waving back her long dark tresses, she was at the gate almost before the tongue of the bell ceased to vibrate. Annabella saw her start, caught the uttered exclamation, and springing from her room, clearing the stairs almost at a bound, in less than a minute was at the side of her cousin. She was quickly followed by the vicar and Mrs. Aumerle, and every member of the household.

A telegraphic message had arrived from Augustine; yes, there was the precious little leaf, which, like the touch of a magician's wand, changed the face of everything around, and flooded the dry, haggard cheek of sorrow with a torrent of grateful tears.

CLIFF COTTAGE, B——, DEVON.

"Safe, thank God! I shall send M—— home to-morrow. I remain here with the earl, who is attacked by brain fever. I have telegraphed to Exeter for Dr. G—— and a nurse.—A. A."

"Brain fever!" exclaimed the countess with a gasp.

"Temporary illness, I trust,—only temporary," said the vicar, from whose heart the weight of a mountain seemed removed. "Augustine, thoughtful as he ever is, has already taken every human means to insure recovery."

"My Reginald shall be left to no nurse; no, no, none shall rob me of one privilege," cried Annabella. "I will be at B—— beside him to-night."

"I will be your escort," said Lawrence Aumerle.

"Oh, take me too!" exclaimed Ida, her dark eyes swimming in tears at the thought of seeing her sister.

"No, no," interrupted Mrs. Aumerle, "numbers are by no means desirable where a man in brain fever is concerned. It is bad enough for your father to have to undertake a long journey, without the whole family hurrying off. You will stay here with me, my dear, and welcome back Mabel to-morrow."

A short time before Ida would have rebelled against a decision so much at variance with her inclinations,—would have remonstrated, or at least have murmured; but she had received too severe a lesson for its impression to be speedily effaced, and

reproaching herself for the sigh which alone betrayed
her disappointment, she hastened up-stairs to prepare
a little parcel of necessaries to be taken to Mabel.

As Ida was putting up, with other articles, the
Bible which she knew that her sister would especially
welcome, she was unexpectedly joined by Mrs
Aumerle.

"You may leave that business to me," said the
lady, with more real kindness of intention than
tenderness of manner; "your father says that it
would be hard not to let you make one of the
party, so you had better get ready for the journey
at once."

Joyful at the permission, Ida hastened to make
her little preparations; and Mrs. Aumerle, as she
packed Mabel's parcel, informed her step-daughter
of the arrangements which she had herself made for
the convenience of all. A messenger had been
promptly despatched to the nearest neighbour who
kept a carriage, to ask the loan of the conveyance to
carry the travellers to the nearest railway station.
Nothing that could insure the comfort of the vicar
was forgotten when his carpet-bag was packed by
the hands of his careful wife; Ida received sundry
injunctions to watch over the health of her father,
and the good housewife took care that the travellers
should not fast on the way.

When the carriage drove away from the door of
the vicarage, with its eager, anxious occupants, Mrs.

Aumerle, following it to the gate, watched it from
thence till it disappeared in a turn of the road. And
thus the woman of sense soliloquised on events, past,
present, and future:—

"How much trouble and misery has been caused
by one act of selfish folly! Because Augustine—
too great a genius, I suppose, to judge like a sensible
man—fancies to roam through the clouds, and take
with him a wilful, disobedient child, while a petulant girl eggs on her husband to follow so absurd
an example, a whole family must be plunged into
terror, grief, and alarm! I felt convinced from the
first that all would end happily enough. Augustine
has easily guided the balloon; it has floated quietly
down at its leisure to some quiet meadow in Devon;
and but for the poor earl's shaken nerves, the whole
affair to those most concerned has been nothing but
a party of pleasure! It is we who have had to
suffer for the senseless folly of others. There's Ida
has been looking like a spectre; and my dear,
excellent husband is first almost crushed with sorrow,
and then hurried off, at half-an-hour's notice, to
escort that half frantic countess to a husband who
will probably refuse to see her! Well, well, I
believe that of all senses common sense is the most
uncommon!" and with a soothing conviction that a
portion, at least, of the rare gift had been bestowed
upon herself, Mrs. Aumerle quietly returned to her
usual avocations.

It was fortunate for Mabel that the morrow's post brought to her step-mother's hands the letter which the young girl had dropped from the balloon. Ida had left a request, that notes addressed to her might in her absence be opened by Mrs. Aumerle, and thus it was that that lady first became aware of some of the perils through which the travellers had passed. Mabel's letter had been picked up in a field and posted by the farmer who had found it, and the touching lines of love and penitence which she had penned in the near prospect of a terrible death, softened in a very great degree the feelings of her step-mother towards her.

"She has had her share of suffering after all," observed the lady, "and we must not be severe upon the poor child. She has had punishment enough for her fault, so I'm content to 'let bygones be bygones.'"

CHAPTER XXVIII.

THE WHEEL TURNS.

"Thus artists melt the sullen ore of lead,
By heaping coals of fire upon its head."
                                    GOLDSMITH.

WHEN the Countess of Dashleigh, with bitter words
of reproach, had departed from the cottage of Bardon,
she left her late entertainers in a state of mind little
to be envied. The unfortunate Cecilia was for the
rest of the day much in the position of one who,
with hands tied, is caged up with a large hornet
which has been irritated, and which goes about
buzzing with evident determination to find or to
make a foe. Everything went wrong with the
doctor, and his daughter was the only being within
reach of the hornet's sting !

Bardon's temper broke out especially at dinner,
where every little luxury which had been prepared
for Annabella served as a provocation to her irritated
host. The unfortunate chicken (a delicacy till lately
almost unknown at the little cottage), could not
have been more denounced as tough, tasteless, and
uneatable, if it had been a roasted owl. The tart-
lets (made surreptitiously by poor Cecilia in the

absence of Mrs. Bates) roused such an angry storm
against all the inventors, makers, and eaters of such
abominable trash, that Cecilia silently resolved that
they should never appear on the table again; she
would rather throw them into the road! Miss
Bardon's gaily tinted bubble of grandeur had
broken, and left behind nothing but bitterness and
—bills !

The fact was that Dr. Bardon was angry with
himself, though a great deal too proud to own it.
He was haunted by the countenance of the unfortunate Dashleigh as he last had seen it in the car, and
had a strong persuasion on his mind that the earl,
in a fit of frenzy, would fling himself out of the
balloon, and be dashed to pieces in the fall ! The
subject of the ascent of the *Eaglet* was one so painful to Bardon that he would endure no allusion to
it ; and Cecilia soon discovered that there was no
method of raising a storm so certain, as that of
uttering aloud the conjectures and apprehensions to
which such an event naturally gave rise. Silence,
particularly on so interesting a subject, was a cruel
penance to the poor lady, to whom gossip was one
of the few remaining pleasures of life, but to that
penance she was obliged to submit as being the
lesser of two evils.

The anxious vicar himself had not passed a more
disturbed night with the images of his child and
his brother breaking his rest, than did the proud

old doctor. Conscience had at length made him miserable, although it had not made him meek. He was no longer stormy, but he was sullen; and he did not even choose to communicate to his daughter his intention of calling on the Aumerles as soon as his breakfast should be concluded, in order to inquire whether anything had been heard of the missing balloon.

The postman, who had just left at the vicarage "The Fairy Lake" for the Countess of Dashleigh, now called at the cottage with a letter. The doctor's correspondents were so very few in number that such an event was sufficiently rare to excite attention; and Bardon's mind was so pre-occupied with the idea of coming misfortune and death, that he turned pale on seeing that the epistle directed to him was sealed and deep-bordered with black.

Cecilia, who had her full allowance of natural curiosity, watched the countenance of her father as he broke open and perused the letter. She saw his colour return, while his eye-brows were elevated as if in surprise; he read the epistle twice without comment, and then silently handed it over to his daughter.

The letter was a formal notification from the executors of the late Thomas Auger, Esq., that that gentleman had, by a will executed but a few days previous to his decease, given and bequeathed the dwelling-house called Nettleby Tower, and the land appertaining thereto, to Timon Bardon, M.D., the only surviving son of their former proprietor; and that he willed also that the said Timon Bardon should be paid from his estate a sum equal to that which had been expended by him in his lawsuit with the testator for the property above mentioned.

Cecilia, almost as much delighted as she was surprised, glanced up eagerly at her father. She read no exultation in his countenance, but rather a thoughtful sorrow, which his daughter could scarcely understand. Could she have penetrated his reflections, they would have appeared somewhat like the following : " Such, then, was the last act of the man whom I hated, over the announcement of whose death I gloated with malignant triumph ! He remembered me on his death-bed; while struggling with the last enemy, he sought to make reparation for a wrong committed years ago, but never forgotten or forgiven by me. Through his sense of justice, I am at length restored to the home and estate of my fathers. Prosperity is sent to me, but through a channel so unexpected, and at a moment so painful, that I scarcely know how to welcome it, for I feel as though I did not deserve it."

" Papa," cried Cecilia, " do you not rejoice ?"

Bardon turned silently away. To compare greater things with less, his were something of the emotions of a child who has justly incurred a parent's displeasure, and who, while awaiting in a spirit of sullen rebellion a further manifestation of wrath, is surprised by a sudden token of love, unexpected as unmerited. The child, if a spark of generous feeling be left in his nature, is more pained by the kindness of his offended parent than he would have been by a sign of anger. His heart is melted; his conscience is touched. Timon Bardon had hardened his heart in adversity; he had girt on the panoply of pride; he had gloried in his powers of endurance, as one ready to do battle with the world, and to trample down all its frivolous distinctions. He had been ever trying to conceal the fact that he was a sad and disappointed man, both from himself and others, by affecting a contempt for all the worldly advantages which Providence had seen fit to deny ; but to have these advantages suddenly restored to him, and at a period when he was conscious,—could not · but be conscious,—that he had merited a Father's chastening rod, had a much more softening effect upon him than would have been produced by adversity's heaviest stroke. The tidings which came in the evening of the safety of the travellers in the *Eaglet*, gave a much keener sense of pleasure to Bardon than had been produced by the news of the morning.

And now we will return to the countess and her companions. The horses of their carriage were urged to speed, yet were they barely in time to catch the train, and the party had scarcely taken their seats before it began to move on. Oh, how Annabella longed to give the wings of her own impatience to the lagging engine! How her yearning spirit realized the complaint,—

> " Miles interminably spread,
> Seem lengthening as I go ! "

Night had closed around before the travellers reached the little station which was nearest to the place of their destination,—a small, lonely post at which the train merely stopped for two minutes to suffer the party to alight.

" Can any conveyance be procured here ?" asked Aumerle of the solitary station official who was assisting to put down their luggage.

" No, sir," was the unsatisfactory reply. " There was a chaise sent here two hours ago for a gentleman who came by last train ; nothing of the kind is to be had here, unless it's ordered aforehand from the town."

" Is that chaise likely to return hither ?"

" Can't say, sir," answered the man. " I believe that it took a doctor and nurse to a place where a nobleman's lying ill, who was picked up to-day from the sea."

" The sea !" echoed the astonished listeners.

" Fallen out of a balloon, as I understand," said the man. " There was a party of three, and they were all saved by one of our fishing-smacks that was just coming in from a cruise."

"Oh, guide us to the place where they are!" exclaimed the countess.

"Can't leave the station, ma'am," replied the official, looking with some curiosity and interest on the pale, eager face on which the light of the gas-lamp fell; "besides, I've not been long at this place, and don't know exactly where the cottage lies."

"What are we to do?" exclaimed Ida.

"Now I think on it," said the station-man, slowly, "the doctor asked me when the last train would go back to Exeter to-night. I take it he's likely to return; and you could have the chaise that brings him."

"When does that train pass?" inquired the vicar.

"Within an hour," replied the man, glancing round at the large clock behind him. "Will not the ladies walk into the waiting-room?—it is better than standing out here on the platform."

"It appears our best course," said the vicar, addressing the countess, "to await here the return of the doctor, and avail ourselves of the only conveyance that seems likely to call here to-night."

"Oh no, no!" exclaimed Annabella, wildly; "every minute of delay is an age in purgatory! The doctor may never come. Augustine will not suffer him to quit Dashleigh for an hour! I wait for no one; I will try to find my way to the cottage;—I go at once, even if I go alone!"

As Annabella remained firm in her resolution, the

party, after gleaning such scanty information as the man at the station could give, and procuring from him a lantern, set out on their dreary way. Perfect darkness is seldom known in Devon on a night in May, but clouds and the absence of the moon rendered the atmosphere unusually obscure. Strange and phantom-like looked the black shadows of their own forms to the travellers, as the glare of the lantern cast them on the chalky cliffs that bordered their road. The path was rough and steep, strewn with stone boulders here and there, which seemed to have rolled down from the rocky heights above.

After a long, toilsome struggle up a gorge, where the countess much needed the aid of the vicar's arm, the party emerged on the summit of a hill, whence in daylight they would have commanded an extensive prospect. Now faint gleams of summer light alone revealed to them by glimpses what appeared to be a wild, rocky valley, sloping down on the left to the sea, the mournful murmur of whose billows came upon the sighing breeze. Viewed by the imperfect light, the scene was very desolate and drear, and in its gloomy sublimity struck a chill to the heart of Annabella.

" It is like the valley of the shadow of death !" she whispered to Ida Aumerle.

" Even were it so, dearest," was the reply, " is it not beyond the dark valley that the land of promise lies ?"

"To those who are sure of a welcome," faltered forth the unhappy countess.

"I think that I hear the sound of wheels," observed the vicar; "yes,—some vehicle is evidently slowly ascending the steep hill before us."

"Surely that of Dr. G—— upon its return," suggested Ida.

The idea made all quicken their steps. Ida's guess had been partially correct; in front was the expected chaise, moving as if towards the station.

As soon as the vehicle was sufficiently near, Mr. Aumerle hailed the driver :—

"Whence do you come, my friend?"

"From Cliff Cottage," replied a rough voice through the darkness, and then the panting of a horse was heard.

"Is it the doctor?" exclaimed Annabella, pressing eagerly forward.

"No," replied the voice. "A gentleman is ill; the doctor is staying the night; I'm to return for him in the morning;" and the speaker cracked his whip as a signal to the weary horse to move forward.

Arrangements were speedily made with the driver by Mr. Aumerle; the conveyance was turned round at the first convenient spot, and in it the ladies and the vicar were soon on their way to the cottage in which the Earl of Dashleigh lay ill.

Few words were interchanged as the travellers descended the rough, and almost precipitous road;

indeed, the violent jolting would, under any circumstances, have rendered conversation impossible. Progress was necessarily slow, and it was some time
before the party reached a lonely, shingle-built
cottage belonging to a fisherman, which stood almost
on the margin of the sea.

There was no need to knock at the low, rude door,
for a quick ear within had caught the sound of
wheels, most unusual in that lonely spot, and the
vicar had scarcely had time to alight, before Mabel
was in the arms of her father!

CHAPTER XXIX.

TWO WORDS.

————

"Teach me to love and to forgive,
    Exact my own defects to scan,
  What others are to feel,—and know myself a man!"
                                                    GRAY.

"To lose thee! oh! to lose thee,—to live on
    And see the sun, not thee! will the sun shine—
  Will the birds sing—flowers bloom, when thou art gone?
    Desolate! desolate!"
                                        BULWER'S KING ARTHUR.

————

"Oh, I was sure that you would come,—quite sure! And Ida—my own precious Ida!" The poor young girl clung to her sister as if they had been parted for years.

"My husband!" exclaimed Annabella, trembling lest terrible news should await her.

"He is much the same, but—"

"Where is he—I will fly to him; I—"

"My dear madam," said the low voice of a stranger, as a tall, bald gentleman in black came forth from the interior of the cottage, with his finger raised to his lip, "may I request that no sound be uttered—my patient is in a state of high fever."

"I will quietly glide up to his room—"

"If, as I suppose, I have the honour of addressing

the Countess of Dashleigh, I trust that she will pardon my strictly forbidding any one but Mr. Aumerle and the nurse from entering the chamber of the earl."

" I am his wife !" murmured Annabella hoarsely.

" It is impossible," said Dr. G——, "that you should meet without a degree of excitement which might endanger the life or the reason of my patient. The earl is in excellent hands ; his friend, and the skilful attendant whom I have provided, will watch him night and day. If any new face were to be seen, I would not be answerable for the consequences."

Dr. G—— had, of course, read "The Precipice and the Peer," and naturally concluded that its authoress.was the last person who could with impunity be admitted into the sick-room of the excited and fevered patient. From the physician's decision there was no appeal, though to Annabella it appeared an intolerable sentence of banishment from the place to which both duty and affection called her. Always ready to rush to a conclusion, the unhappy wife was convinced that it was the just resentment of Dashleigh against her, that rendered her of all beings in the world the one whose presence he could not endure. Utterly prostrate and helpless in her sorrow, the countess left to Ida all care for the arrangements of the night. To herself it was nothing where she slept, or whether she ever should sleep again ; she was like a flower so crushed and bruised that it will never more unfold its petals to the sun.

The rude cottage of the fisherman offered wretched accommodation for so large a party. The earl occupied one of the two little bed-rooms which were reached by a ladder-like staircase; in the other—an apartment not ten feet square, with bare rafters, sloping roof, and single-paned window engrained with dust and sea salt, and incapable of being opened—the countess and her cousins passed the night. The gentlemen had to content themselves with the bare floor of the kitchen below, redolent of the scent of fish, and garlanded with nets and tackle,—an accommodation which they shared with their rough, weather-beaten, but hospitable host.

Annabella and Ida were so much exhausted by previous excitement, fatigue, and want of rest, that even in the miserable hovel they might have slept deeply and long, had it not been for the sounds from the next room, almost as distinctly heard through the slight partition as if the apartments had been one. It was agony to the countess to hear the moans of the fevered sufferer, or the wild words uttered in delirium. Ida passed the night in vain endeavours to soothe and calm a wounded spirit, while the weary Mabel peacefully slumbered beside them, unconscious of what was passing around. It was almost as great a relief to Ida as to her afflicted cousin when the morning broke at length, and welcome silence on the

other side of the partition told that the sufferer had
sunk to rest.

Augustine Aumerle, after watching for hours at
the bedside of the earl, whom he alone had any
power to soothe in the paroxysms of his terrible
malady, now resigned his post to the nurse, and descending the steep, narrow staircase, went forth to
calm and refresh his spirit by a brief walk on the
shore of the sea,—that sea in which he had so lately
expected to find a grave. As he stood gazing on
the bright expanse of waters, and enjoying the fresh
morning breeze that, as it rippled the surface of the
sea, also brought back the hue of health to his pale and
careworn cheek, he was joined by Lawrence Aumerle.

Kindly greeting was exchanged between the
brothers; questions were asked and replies were
given, and then a silence succeeded. Something
seemed pressing on the heart of each, to which the
lip would not give ready utterance. Augustine was
the first to speak, but he did so without looking at
his brother; he rather seemed to be watching the
sea-bird that lightly floated on the wave.

"Lawrence, you remember the evening when we
conversed together in your study?"

"I have often thought of it since."

"And so have I," said Augustine; "I thought of
it when I believed that there was but one step between me and death,—when I expected in a brief
space to be in that world where we shall know even

as we are known,—where ours will not be the wild
guess, but the absolute certainty,—not the wild
grasping at the shadow, but the laying hold on the
substance of truth."

Lawrence fixed his eyes anxiously upon his
brother, but did not interrupt him by a word.

" You said that experience is the growth of time.
Lawrence, I have, then, lived an age in the last forty
hours.   A wide view of both heaven and earth is
gained from the terrible height that I reached ! "

" Common experience is the growth of time," said
the vicar ; " but spiritual experience—"

" Give it in the words of inspiration," interrupted
Augustine ; " I shall no longer ask you to put aside
that solemn evidence, even for a moment.   *Tribulation worketh patience ; and patience, experience.*"

" *And experience, hope ;*" cried the vicar.   " Oh,
my brother !—that blessed hope shed abroad in the
heart by the knowledge that Christ *died for the
ungodly*, that hope that alone *maketh not ashamed*,
is it—oh! is it your own ?"

Augustine silently pressed the hand that had been
unconsciously extended towards him; it was his only
reply to the question.   Without another sentence
being uttered the brothers turned their steps in the
direction of the cottage.   But while pacing the
shingley beach, Augustine was mentally subscribing
to the confession of one of the brightest geniuses
of earth,—that he had hitherto been but as a child

gathering pebbles on the shore of the great ocean of truth; while the vicar was raising to God, from the depths of a grateful heart, a thanksgiving for prayer answered at the very time when, and through the very trial by which his earthly happiness had appeared crushed and destroyed! He was proving, as so many saints have proved, that—

> " God's purposes will ripen fast,
> Unfolding every hour;
> The bud may have a bitter taste,
> But sweet will be the flower!"

As no object could be answered by the prolonged stay of Mr. Aumerle and Mabel in the over-crowded cottage, they departed on that day for their home. The countess could not endure to quit the spot, and Ida remained to bear her company, while Augustine resumed his watch by his suffering friend.

Day after day the once proud Earl of Dashleigh lay on a pallet-bed in the fisherman's rude hovel, mind and body alike prostrated by the fever induced by the fearful trials which he had endured. He was passing indeed through a burning fiery furnace, but its flame was consuming the dross which had largely mixed with a nobler metal. When the powers of good and evil contend together for the dominion over a human soul, it is as in the battles of earth; dark and painful traces are often left behind of the conflict, conquest is not attained without suffering. Never, perhaps, is the strife more painful than when the enemy to be subdued is pride! Then how often

R

a merciful Providence sends humiliation, anguish, disgrace, first to rouse the soul to a sense of its danger,
and then to aid it in the perilous war! From how
much of suffering is exempted the *meek and quiet
spirit* that has calmly laid down the shackles of
pride, not left them till some loving yet terrible dis-
pensation should wrench them away from the bleed-
ing soul !

Annabella was deeply humbled ; there was some
danger that depression might with her sink into
hopeless despondency. Her ardent and volatile disposition was ever prone to extremes, and she could
not believe it possible that her proud lord could ever
forgive one who had wounded his dignity so deeply,
—one whose indiscretion had so nearly cost him his
life ! The forced inaction to which she had to submit greatly increased the trial to Annabella. If it
had been possible for her to have done or suffered
anything in order to repair the evil that she had
wrought, she would have contemplated its effects
with less overwhelming remorse. Had the countess
belonged to the Church of Rome, she would have
wasted her strength with fasting, lacerated her flesh
by the scourge, or gone on some painful pilgrimage
in the hope of redeeming her fault. As it was, she
had to sit still—useless, helpless, receiving from time
to time tidings of her husband's varying state from
the lips of ministering strangers ! Annabella's spirit
might have altogether sunk under the lengthened

trial, but for the support of Ida's calmer and more chastened spirit, which had itself found its stay on the Rock of Ages.

On the sixth day of Dashleigh's illness, his wife received from her home a small packet, containing the little pocket-book which had been her own earliest gift to her betrothed. The beautiful remembrance had been accidentally discovered at no great distance from the letter which Mabel had dropped; but its comparative weight had made it fall with an impetus that had half imbedded it in the sod. Easily identified by the coronet and name upon the shield, which marked it as the property of the unfortunate nobleman, with whose fate the county was ringing, it had been forwarded to Dashleigh Hall, and thence—still stained and clotted with dust and mud—it had been sent on by her servants to the countess.

Annabella gazed on the book for some moments without daring to unfasten the clasp. The sight of that little gift brought with it a crowd of recollections of the time when wedded life had lain before fancy's eye as a bright, golden-clasped book, on whose yet blank pages hope, pleasure, and love, would trace nothing but sentences of joy! Why was it that the leaves of that life had been blistered and blotted with tears,—that the gold had been tarnished, the beauty marred, and that the once joyous bride now dreaded even to look upon what that book might contain!

"Open it for me, Ida, dearest," murmured Annabella faintly; "I tremble to behold what his fingers may have traced in that terrible hour!"

Ida silently obeyed, kneeling at the side of her unhappy cousin, whose cold hand rested upon her shoulder. Ida turned slowly leaf after leaf. There were various memoranda in the book, evidently written at an earlier period—addresses of friends, names of books, engagements for days long passed. Little of interest or importance could attach to entries such as these. But almost at the end of the book, on a page otherwise blank, appeared two words in pencil, traced evidently by a hand that had shaken from weakness, excitement, or emotion. The words were barely legible, but such as they were Ida with tremulous eagerness pointed them out to her friend. Annabella caught the book from her hand, pressed it convulsively to her lips, and while her eyes overflowed with tears and her heart with thanksgiving, repeated again and again the two blessed words which spoke *forgiveness* and *peace !*

Even while the young wife's tears were still flowing, a gentle tap was heard at the door. Ida went and unclosed it; there was a low whispering sound, and then the maiden returned to her cousin with a gentle smile on her face as she said, laying her hand on that of the countess, " It is my uncle, dearest ; he comes to bring you good tidings. The earl is greatly better,—has been speaking to him,—has been questioning him of you ; he knows— "

" Knows that I am here !" exclaimed Annabella, starting eagerly from her seat.

"Yes, and wishes to see you,—nay, dearest, nay you must be calm,—for his sake you must still this wild excitement ! Remember that he is still very weak,—remember the danger of a relapse !"

" I am quite calm," replied the young countess, collecting herself by a strong effort, though her quivering voice still betrayed her emotion ; " I will do nothing to agitate my lord,—he shall not even hear a word from my lips,—but oh ! the bliss if I may once—but once hear from his those precious words, *forgiveness* and *peace !*"

With soft, noiseless step she glided to the low rough-hewn door which opened into the room of her husband. Gently Annabella pushed it ajar, and entered with a throbbing heart, and a mien as reverential and timid as if she were approaching some solemn fane. That low dark room, with uncarpeted floor, unpapered walls, furniture coarse and scanty, contained what she now felt was all the world to her.

No human friend intruded his presence on the sacredness of that scene which ever after, to the memory of Annabella, hallowed that fisherman's hut. When the penitent wife knelt in lowly contrition by the pallet of a husband so narrowly rescued from the jaws of the grave, and listened breathlessly to the feeble accents which told her that the past was can-

celled,—that she was dear as ever to him still, angels
may have looked on rejoicing as upon a prodigal's re-.
turn, for no looming shadow darkened the holy
radiance of returning peace and love, no discord jarred
on the harmony of wedded souls,—the demon of pride
was not there !

CHAPTER XXX.

THE SPIRIT LAID.

" From Nature's weeping earth more fair appears,
So should good works succeed repentant tears ! "

GLORIOUSLY poured down the fervid rays of a July
sun, colouring the peach on the wall, swelling the rich
fig under its clustering leaves, ripening the purple
grape, and over the corn fields throwing a mantle of
gold ! No longer in the fisherman's hovel, but reclining on a sofa in the countess's splendid boudoir,
we find the Earl of Dashleigh, yet pale from recent
illness ; the outline of the sunken cheek, the violet
tint beneath the eyes, the whiteness of the transparent skin, tell of suffering severe and protracted, but
health and strength are returning to his frame, while
to the restored invalid lately released from the con-
finement of a sick room—

" The common air, the earth, the skies,
To him are opening paradise ! "

By the softened light which steals in through the
green venetians, the earl has been whiling away the
languid, luxurious hour of noon by perusing a volume
of light literature, in which he has found great

amusement ; that volume, bound in violet and gold,
is now lying on the sofa beside him ; we recognise in
it "THE FAIRY LAKE," written by the Countess of
Dashleigh.

Annabella is seated on a low ottoman beside her
lord. She has been listening with pleased attention
to his remarks and comments upon her work.

"Perhaps, after all," observes Dashleigh, laying his
hand on the book, "it *is* hard to restrict to a few
that which might afford pleasure to the many, and
to deprive the young authoress of the praise and the
fame which publication would bring her."

"O Reginald!" replies his wife with glistening
eyes, "your praise to me outweighs that of the world,
and empty fame is nothing in comparison to a husband's heart ! It would pain me if any eye but yours
should ever look on that which I must ever regard
as a monument of my own disobedience."

Annabella's manner towards her husband has
undergone a change since their re-union in the fisherman's cottage. She is gradually resuming her play-
fulness of conversation, and the wit in which the earl
delights still sparkles for his amusement ; but there is
more, far more of submission to his authority, and of
deference to his wishes in her demeanour ; Annabella no
longer desires to forget that her vow was not only
to love, but to obey.

This change is chiefly owing to that which has
passed over the earl himself. His spirit by intense

suffering has been purified, exalted, refined. That respect which he once claimed on account of his rank is yielded readily on account of his character. Annabella had been disposed to ridicule a dignity that rested on an empty title; her spirit of opposition had been roused, and she had gloried in showing herself above the meanness of aristocratic pride, conscious of a loftier claim to the world's regard than a coronet or a pedigree could give. But if the countess still knows herself to be superior to her husband in intellectual attainments, in moral qualifications she now feels herself far his inferior. Annabella has a quick perception of character, an intuitive reverence for what is solid and real; when she sees beneficence free from ostentation, purity of language and life adopted, not because the reverse would disgrace a peer, but because it would be unworthy of a Christian, she renders the natural homage of an ingenuous heart to virtue, and obedience and tender affection follow in the track of respect.

The conversation has taken a new turn. The earl and his wife have fallen into a train of discourse on some of the occurrences which have been related in preceding chapters. Annabella has now no concealment from her husband, and his gentleness invites her confidence.

" It appears, my love," remarked Dashleigh, " that you quitted the home of the Bardons with scant ceremony and little courtesy."

"He had deserved none," replied Annabella, with something of her old haughtiness in her tone, for very bitter were the memories connected with Timon Bardon.

"There is but one man," pursued the earl, "who, as far as I know, entertains any feeling of resentment against me, or has any just cause to do so. That man is Dr. Bardon."

"It is you who have just cause for resentment against him," said the countess.

"His pride and mine clashed together, and like the collision of flint and steel produced the angry spark which set his spirit in a flame. But, Annabella, I now desire to be at peace with all men. I have never returned the doctor's visit,—you and I will do so to-day."

Annabella opened her large eyes so wide at a proposition so unexpected, as to raise a smile on the lips of the earl.

"You think that I am still too proud to let the red liveries of the Dashleighs be seen at the door of Mill Cottage ?"

"If you were to invade that little nest," said the countess, "you would find that the birds had flown. Do you not remember that Dr. Bardon is now the proprietor of Nettleby Tower ?"

"Ah ! I recollect—by Auger's will, was it not ?" replied Dashleigh, raising his thin hand to his brow. "But this need make no difference in our arrange-

ment for a visit. We will order the carriage in the
cool of the eve, and drive over to wish the old man
and his daughter joy on their return to the family
mansion."

Annabella turned upon her husband a look of admiration and love. She knew how much it must
cost him to make the first step towards reconciliation
with a man who had wronged, hated, and insulted
him. Never, even in the earliest days of their union,
had Dashleigh possessed such influence over the affections of his young wife, as he gained by the simple,
unostentatious act which marked a conquest over
Pride and self.

The sun was sloping towards the west, bathing
earth and sky in the rich glory of his streaming rays,
changing the clouds into floating islands of roses, and
lighting up a little river which flowed through the
landscape, till it glittered like a thread of gold, as
Timon Bardon led a party of guests, comprising all
the family of the Aumerles, to the summit of his grey
old tower, to survey the extensive and beautiful
prospect.

Many a word of admiration was spoken as the
vicar and his party moved from one spot to another,
finding new beauties wherever they gazed. Cecilia,
elegantly dressed as became the lady of the mansion,
appeared in her glory, doing the honours of the
place to her guests. If anything tended in the least
degree to damp her delight, it was her perception

that the practical eye of Mrs. Aumerle (notwithstanding sundry improvements in the dwelling
wrought out under Miss Bardon's direction), had
detected many an unsightly heap of rubbish, many
an unfurnished and dreary chamber, many a defaced
cornice and broken pane, at variance with the notions
of comfort and neatness entertained by the vicar's wife.

Ida and Mabel, who had more poetry in their
nature than had fallen to the lot of Mrs. Aumerle,
and who delighted in whatever recalled to their
minds grand images of the days of chivalry, saw in
the marks of dilapidation but the footprints of ages
gone by, and in imagination peopled the grass-grown
court and the mouldering battlements with mailed
knights, bold archers, and the fair maidens whose
charms had been sung by minstrel and bard in the
time of the old Plantagenets.

"That little grey dot yonder, is it not—" Mabel
began, and paused, for Cecilia, whom she was addressing, looked as if she did not wish to see it.

"Yes, that is Mill Cottage," said the doctor in
a tone more loud and decided even than usual;
"the place where the master of Nettleby Tower dug
out his own potatoes in his garden, and the lady—"

"And that must be Dashleigh Hall," interrupted
Mabel, wishing to effect a diversion, for it was evident
that while the doctor's pride made him rather glory
in his late poverty, that of Miss Bardon rendered
her desirous to forget the days of her humiliation.

But Mabel's diversion was very ill-chosen. At the mention of the name "Dashleigh," the doctor's countenance, which had been wearing an expression far more complacent than that habitual to his leonine features, changed to one dark and louring, the index of the gloomy passions that reigned within. Mabel saw not the change, for her eyes were fixed upon the distant prospect, but it was witnessed by Augustine and Ida, who exchanged glances with each other,—the gentle girl's significant of regret, the uncle's of indignation. "Is not the black drop wrung out from that proud heart yet?" was the mental comment of Augustine.

"Has not this house the repute of being haunted?" asked Ida, in order to turn the doctor's thoughts into a different channel.

"Old women and young fools say that it is so still," replied Timon Bardon gruffly.

"O! Papa," lisped Cecilia, who had no inclination to acknowledge herself as coming under either of these denominations, "you know what strange noises are heard every night!"

"Creaking of doors, cracking of old timber, the wind whistling away in the chimneys!"

"Well, I confess," said Cecilia, with a little affected laugh, "that delightful as the tower is on a summer's day like this, I shall not care to wander much through its long echoing corridors on a dark winter's night. Mr. Aumerle," she continued, ad-

dressing Augustine, who was leaning on the stone
parapet, and gazing down with an abstracted air;
"you who know everything, do you know of no
charm to lay the bad spirits that are said to haunt
ancient houses?"

"I am afraid," replied Augustine gravely, "that
such spirits are wont to haunt new houses as well
as old ones, and that it needs more knowledge than
philosophy can teach to give us the power to lay
them."

Cecilia looked puzzled at the enigmatical reply,
but before she had time to ask for a solution, Mabel
interrupted the conversation by suddenly exclaiming,
"Surely that is the Dashleigh's carriage that has
just turned the corner of the hill!"

"We have stayed long enough on this tower," said
the doctor, averting his eyes from the direction in
which those of Mabel were turned; "let us descend
to the court."

His suggestion, which sounded like a command,
was followed at once by his guests; poor Cecilia
heaved a sigh at the thought that once she might
have indulged a hope that the gay carriage with its
dashing bays might be bound for Nettleby Tower.
"After all that has happened," she reflected sadly,
"that is impossible now!"

The descent of the long winding stairs, whose
steep, rude, age-worn steps were only dimly lighted
by narrow slits cut here and there in the massive

stone wall, required both caution and time. Ere
Bardon, who was the last of the party, had emerged
from the low-browed door which opened into the
court-yard, the bridge across the moat had been
crossed, and the Earl and Countess of Dashleigh
were already exchanging kindly greetings with the
foremost of the Aumerles.

The stern old doctor was more startled by the
unexpected appearance at his threshold of visitors
such as these, than he could have been by any appari-
tion in his old haunted tower. Mingled feelings
of surprise, shame, remorse, and gratified pride
struggled together in his bosom, as his eye met that
of the nobleman from whose house he had turned
with emotions of such vindictive wrath—words of
such fiery passion ! Had Bardon's newly recovered
estate depended upon his making such an effort, the
proud man could not have bowed his spirit to the
humiliation of visiting the earl ; and yet the nobleman had come to him,—to him who had so meanly,
so cruelly avenged one slighting sentence accidentally
overheard !

Dashleigh saw the surprise, the embarrassment
written on the face of the haughty Bardon,—he felt
the delicacy of his own position, and resolutely
breaking through what would once have been the
inseparable barrier of reserve, he advanced two or
three steps towards the doctor, and while a painful
flush mantled over his wasted features, frankly held

out his hand.   That hand was grasped—was wrung
—but in silence; the proud man felt himself con-
quered; and from that hour the evil spirit of enmity
between the two opponents was laid for ever!

Can I add that the dark tyrant Pride had for
ever yielded up his empire, that he never again
whispered his evil suggestions to those who so long
had worn his chain?

Alas! I dare not thus violate probability, or sacrifice the great truth of which this fiction is the
fanciful vehicle.   The contest against Pride is a
life-long campaign.   From the time when he breathed
ambition to Eve in the words, *Ye shall be as gods*, or
roused in the heart of the first murderer the hatred
which stained his hand with the blood of a more
favoured brother, the influence of pride over our
fallen race has been fearful, too often fatal!   I have
but sketched him in some of his forms,—of how
many have I not even attempted to trace the outline!   Pride of purse, Pride of person, family Pride,
national Pride, the Pride that draws the trigger of
the duellist, that tightens the grasp of the oppressor,
and, perhaps worst of all, spiritual Pride, which
brings Satan before even the saintly in the guise of
an angel of light!   Let some more powerful pencil
draw these, till conscience start at the portrait of
the demon who seeks the house that is *cleansed and
garnished*, nor comes alone, but brings with him

ambition, dissension, jealousy, hatred, and other dark ministers of death.

Reader! have you recognised Pride as an evil, have you struggled with him as a foe? Look to your soul and see if it bear not the mark of his galling chain. If the fetter be on it still, oh! with the strength of faith and the energy of prayer, burst it, even as Samson burst the green withes with which a secret enemy had bound him! Or, to change the metaphor, if you feel the proud spirit within, like the inflated sphere of the æronaut, ready to bear you aloft to a cloudy and perilous height, whence you will look down on your fellow-creatures, stop not to dally with danger, persuade not yourself that the peril is unreal, but resolute as one who knows that life and more than life is at stake, clip the soaring wing of the *Eaglet,*—cut the cords of your balloon!

> Proud,—and of what? poor, vain, and helpless worm,
> Crawling in weakness through thy life's brief term,
> Yet filled with thoughts presumptuous, bold, and high,
> As though thy grovelling soul could scan the sky,—
> As though thy wisdom, which cannot foreshow
> What *one* day brings of coming weal or woe,
> Could pierce the depths of far futurity,
> And all the winged shafts of fate defy!
>
> Art proud of riches? of the glittering dust
> Each day *may* rob thee of, and one day *must;*
> When mines of wealth will purchase no delay,
> When dust to dust must turn, and clay to clay,
> And nought remain to thee, of all possessed,
> Save one dark cell in earth's unconscious breast?
> Or proud of power? on this little ball
> Some petty tract may thee its master call,
> Some fellow-mortals, bending lowly down,
> Bask in thy smile, or tremble at thy frown

Great in the world's eyes, in thine own more great,
How swells thy breast with conscious pride elate!

And art thou great? lift up—lift up thine eyes,
Survey the heavens, gaze into the skies;
View the fair worlds that glitter o'er thy head,
Orb above orb in bright succession spread,
Beyond the reach of sight, the power of thought: -
Then turn thy gaze to earth, and thou art—nought
The globe itself a speck—an atom; thou —
Oh! child of dust, shall pride exalt thee now?
In one thing only thou mayst glory still,
And let exulting joy thy bosom fill;
Glory in this,—and what is all beside,
That for this worm, this atom,—Jesus died

Does conscious genius fire thy haughty mind,
Genius that raises man above his kind,—
The lofty soul that soars on wing of fire,
While crowds at distance marvel and admire?
Oh! while the charmed world pays her homage just,
Remember, every *talent* is a *trust*,
A treasure God doth to thy care confide,
A cause for gratitude, but none for pride!
If thou that precious talent misapply
To spread the power of infidelity,
To strew with flowers the path which sinners tread,
To hide one treacherous snare by Satan spread,
How blest—how great compared to thee—that man
Whose life obscurely ends as it began,
To whose meek soul no knowledge e'er was given,
Save that, of all most high,—that guides to heaven!
Far as the sun's pure radiance, streaming bright,
Transcends the glow-worm's dim and fading light,
The wisdom to his soul vouchsafed from high
Exceeds the earth-born fires that flash—and die!

Oh! where shall pride securely harbour then,
Where urge his claims to rule the minds of men?
Blest Eden knew him not,—where all was fair—
Where all was faultless—pride abode not there! ·
The glorious angels are above his sway,
Their bliss to minister—to serve—obey;
We, only we, poor children of a day,
Tread haughtily the ground for our sakes curst,
And wear with pride the chains our Surety burst!

Would that the world could know and truly prize
That which is great in the Creator's eyes!
The poor man, bending o'er his scanty store,
Who, with God's presence blest, desires no more,
Who feels his sins—his weakness,—though his ways
Be just and pure beyond all *human* praise;

Whose humble thoughts well with his prayer accord,
"Have mercy upon me, a sinner, Lord!"
Who, heir of an eternal, heavenly throne,
Rests all his hopes on Christ, and Christ alone!
Wisest of men—for he alone is wise,—
Richest of men—secure his treasure lies,—
Greatest of men—his mansion is on high;
His father—God,—his rest—Eternity!

BIBLIOLIFE

Old Books Deserve a New Life
www.bibliolife.com

Did you know that you can get most of our titles in our trademark **EasyScript**[TM] print format? **EasyScript**[TM] provides readers with a larger than average typeface, for a reading experience that's easier on the eyes.

Did you know that we have an ever-growing collection of books in many languages?

Order online:
www.bibliolife.com/store

Or to exclusively browse our **EasyScript**[TM] collection:
www.bibliogrande.com

At BiblioLife, we aim to make knowledge more accessible by making thousands of titles available to you – quickly and affordably.

Contact us:
BiblioLife
PO Box 21206
Charleston, SC 29413